# HOOT'S
# WISDOM NUGGETS

## TO HELP YOU BECOME A

# SUPER SALESMAN

# HOOT GIBSON

36hoot@gmail.com

# PROLOGUE

Of all the books I have read on selling, I have never read one like this. I hope I can find the words to describe my thoughts! As I read the manuscript, I thought this is the best book, by far, that I have ever read on the "how to" of selling.

I especially liked the fact that it tells you what to do in every selling opportunity. It was so easy to read and remember because of the many examples told in short stories of situations encountered and how to handle them.

How I wish I had had it during my fifty plus years of buying, operating, and selling various businesses. However, as Hoot said in his book, you don't get a "do-over!"

I believe a person with average intelligence, with this book as their guide, would find it hard not to succeed. It is so powerful, yet simply presented. All you would have to do is just do what is taught in this book.

If it is your heart's desire to be happy and successful in life, this book could be your outline. It is my opinion that this book is a masterpiece on how to sell.

It explains in detail every step you will need to know and do to become an outstanding salesman, and I believe you will enjoy following those steps.

If this book excites you as much as it does me, and if you have the desire and enthusiasm to learn and do what it teaches, I believe you will accomplish far more than you ever believed possible. It would be hard to do otherwise.

Like Hoot said, "There is no limit to what you can accomplish."

I have so much more to say but am finding it difficult to find the words. Therefore I will simply say you will be so proud of yourself and happy when you achieve all that this book will help you to accomplish.

*-J. V. "Bud" Dasher, Jr.*
*businessman, entrepreneur, philanthropist*
**(Endowed Dasher Memorial Heart Center,**
**Valdosta, Georgia)**

# TABLE OF CONTENTS

# FOREWORD

After reading the manuscript for your sales book, I must say that you have a very effective writing style. As I went down the pages, the 52 nuggets and 20 chapters, I enjoyed your style and content.

Although I have an undergraduate degree from Ohio State University in "Mechanical Engineering" and a degree from the University of Alabama in "Computer Science" and "Marketing" and know a lot about marketing, technology, and engineering, I knew little about sales especially real estate sales.

After reading your collections of anecdotes and examples of sales processes and procedures, I gained a new understanding and respect for the sales profession and especially what it takes to become a top salesman. I think your expressed knowledge and experience in sales can be applied to a broad range of sales activities in any field.

I find your book to be a valuable and effective training manual for anyone who wants to be a top salesman. While *Hoot's Wisdom Nuggets to Help You Become a Super Salesman* is focused on real estate, it appears the precepts you present can be applied to any sales activities, as well as personal relationships.

I was very impressed with the manuscript and found myself more informed about sales and sales techniques. I believe it would have been very helpful to me even in my career as an engineer. I would recommend it to salesmen in any field. Having this book would give them a great advantage over their peers.

I am pleased you shared it with me.

*-Jack A. Riehle*

# INTRODUCTION

This book is a guide on how to sell. Much of it is written about selling real estate. Even so, the concepts apply to all kinds of selling. They also apply to life in general. The first chapter has some important information about selling that you will need to know. However, most of it is about my background. If you are anxious to begin, you may want to skip Chapter One for now; you can come back and read it later.

Most, if not all states have laws and disclosure regulations to regulate the real estate industry. These laws and regulations are constantly changing. It is the ideas and concepts in this book that you should learn. You can always modify them to comply with the current laws and disclosure regulations of your state.

This book will give you all the ideas and concepts you will ever need in learning how to sell. It doesn't matter what you are selling. Selling is selling! The more you study and learn, the better, easier, richer, and successful your life will be because all of life involves selling.

Some of the stories, anecdotes, and examples in this book may not apply today. However, that is how we did it back then in what you might call the "Stone age." You can make changes to fit today's situations.

It is not all about money, even though that is an important part. Learn what this book teaches, and your success will be much more than you ever expected.

You will discover that a Super Salesman is not necessarily a better salesman than you. He will not work harder or longer, but he will have lots of enthusiasm and a strong work ethic. He will not be charismatic knowing exactly what to say at all times.

However, he will have an intensity that is hard to

explain. He will be someone who works differently. In this book, you will learn what that difference is and how to apply it.

Selling is usually thought of as selling a product. It could be an automobile, vacuum cleaner, real estate, insurance policy, or some other item.

It doesn't always have to be a product being sold. It can be an idea or concept. It can be tangible or intangible. It can be a young man selling a girl on going out on a date. It can be a buyer selling the seller on accepting a lower price. Does that sound confusing? Not to worry, all these parts of selling are discussed in the book.

Salesmen can be divided into several categories. One is the "order-taker," and that is exactly what they do. They take orders. I have seen some order-takers go beyond what is expected of them, thus becoming a "true-salesman," which is another category. They are the ones who make things happen.

A "true-salesman" is honest, ethical, and tries to do what is in the best interest of the buyer. Obviously, that is good. His job will become easier over time as he builds a following who will return to buy again and refer others to him.

Another category is the "high-pressure salesman." You have seen them. They try to pressure the buyer into doing what is in the salesman's best interest. Not good!

Beginning in the first chapter, I will give you some of my background. Chapter two is where the how to of selling really starts. From that point on, everything will be leading up to the last chapter where it all comes together.

This is a book of experience and knowledge, not theory. I spent over 40 years learning and obtaining these ideas and concepts. You can learn them in a few hours of reading, studying, and a few years of putting them into practice.

Of course, reading this book doesn't mean you will be a top salesman in a few weeks. However, by implementing what this book teaches, you will be amazed at how quickly these ideas will become useful in helping you to become a top salesman in any area.

If you have the desire and drive to read, to learn, and to do, your success will be far greater than mine. I didn't have the benefit of the knowledge and experience discussed in this book in my beginning.

You can achieve an income of several hundred thousand to over a million dollars a year. Yes and you can even do it in a small town.

As you read this book, you may become excited and decide to implement all these ideas immediately. If you do, I predict you will fail. You probably didn't expect me to say that but it's true. Whether it is this or any other book, video, or seminar, there is a method you must use to study and to learn.

What you must do is pick one concept or idea at a time. Work on that idea until it becomes second nature to the point it becomes instinctive so you won't even have to think about it.

That is why I have 52 Wisdom Nuggets. If you pick one Nugget to concentrate on each week, in one year you will be well ahead of your competitors and on your way to success as a Super Salesman.

The three paragraphs above you just read are three of the most important paragraphs in the book. Because of their importance, I have placed a reminder in the last chapter for you to come back, and read them again.

*-Hoot Gibson, Author*

# CHAPTER ONE
## My Background

This chapter is your introduction to my life and why this book was written. It explains why I believe, if done correctly, a career in selling can be awesome. My intention is to show that it doesn't matter where you start; it is where you finish that is important. I also believe you should know something about this author's "not so great beginnings." It's a testimony that you can do the same or better.

As I said in the Introduction, this chapter is mainly about my background. If you are not interested in that, you can **skip to Chapter Two**. However, you may want to come back, and read this chapter later because there is some important information about selling in it.

To begin I will tell you how I got the name "Hoot." You need to know the original "Hoot Gibson" was a famous cowboy, rodeo star, and stuntman in the early days of silent and talking movies. His real name was Edmund Richard Gibson. If you are interested in how he got the nickname "Hoot" you can look it up on the INTERNET.

All my life people have asked me questions about my name. First, "How did you get that name?" The next question, "Are you the original Hoot Gibson?" The last question is, "Do you have a middle name?"

Here are the answers: My father was an avid cowboy fan. Therefore, when my mother was pregnant with me, he announced, boy or girl, the name will be "Hoot." Sure enough, he held true to his word. In answer to the next question, I must be the original because it is my real name but only a nickname of the "Hoot" who started it all. The last question, "Do you have a middle name?" Who needs a middle name with a name like "Hoot?"

Recently a young man I know came up to me in the gym and said he was considering getting his real estate license so he could sell real estate. Because I am a retired real estate broker, I gave him a few pointers on how to sell.

He asked me where he could get more information. After thinking for a few moments, I told him he would have to learn by experience. I do not know of a single source, school, seminar, video, or book that would give him the knowledge and experience I learned during my career of 40 plus years as an Air Force recruiter/salesman and real estate salesman/broker. This young man's question got me to thinking. All the knowledge and experience I gained over those years should not be lost. Therefore, I decided to write this book.

In the past, people have said, "Hoot you should write a book." They knew I had accumulated a considerable amount of knowledge and experience as a successful real estate salesman/broker. Previously I had thought of writing a book. However, it seemed like such a daunting task. The most writings I had ever done were letters to the editor of my local newspaper.

Therefore, after thinking about it, I decided to simply tell my story, my life experiences, and the lessons I learned over the years as a salesman. Not being sure where to begin, I decided to start at the beginning of my adult life, giving you a little of my background and experiences before I got into sales. First, let me discuss some terms I will use and put in a disclaimer so as not to be accused of plagiarizing.

I wish I could say every thought and idea in this book

originally came from me; however, I cannot. Many, perhaps most have come from my own experiences. Others, I may have read in a book, heard in a seminar, or it could have come from just talking or brainstorming with other sales people, plus my life experiences. Then I refined this information by trial and error over a period of 40 plus years.

I would like to give credit to everyone who contributed to my knowledge. However, I do not know or remember who contributed what. Also, I am aware that terms like "buyer", "seller", "client," and "customer" each has a different and distinct meaning.

However, to make the writing and the reading flow easier, and for convenience, sometimes I may say "customer" for any one of them. I also may use the singular term when it includes a couple or the plural when it should be singular. Rather than be politically correct, I may say "he" or "his" when it should have been "she" or "her." The same thing applies when I say "salesman" instead of "saleswoman."

Now back to my story. My family moved a lot when I was a small child. Sometimes we lived several miles out in the country. One time we lived in Ocala, Florida, another time in Panama City, Florida. During those times, we didn't have electricity. Imagine the ramifications!

There was no clothes washer or dryer. We used a scrub board to wash our clothes and a solar dryer to dry them. We called it a clothes line. Even if you had electricity, there was no such thing as television. The whole family took baths once a week in a galvanized #3 wash tub. The youngest was the last to bathe. Lucky me, in a family of six, I was next to last.

At night we used kerosene lamps for lighting. We

mowed the grass with a hand-pushed lawn mower. When the gasoline power mowers came along, they were fondly referred to as "dog crap slingers." When I was eight years old, my family settled down in the Big Bend of Florida in the small town of Perry. I lived there until I graduated from high school and joined the military.

Just before graduating from high school in 1954 my best friend said, "Hoot, we should go into the air conditioning business." He said, "One day almost everyone will have air conditioning in their homes." Imagine that! At the time, I thought he was out of his mind.

I thought only huge department stores, in large cities, have air conditioners. I didn't believe people would ever have them cooling their homes; so for me, air conditioning installation or repair was out of the question. Years earlier, I never dreamed people would actually have toilets and a bathroom built into their homes, but they did. So, don't ask me to predict the future.

Back then most kids didn't think of going to college. That is unless they were going into a profession that required a college degree, such as teaching, medicine, engineering, etc. Higher education was not all that important. There were plenty of jobs to be had without a college education.

It was only a few years earlier that almost no one had refrigerators; we had ice boxes. The iceman delivered ice to our door several times a week. That all changed after the end of the Second World War.

Washers, dryers, refrigerators, freezers, and other modern day conveniences began to appear. Technical jobs were just beginning to become more plentiful. Because of that, technical schools became more popular. They trained people for many of the jobs that were available.

Some of those jobs included appliance repairman, small or large engine repairman, electrician, plumber, painter, clerk, truck driver, barber, and construction worker. Also, in our county there was a large pulp mill that hired many from my graduating class.

One job called "common laborer" included being a ditch digger. We did it with shovels back then. You may be surprised to know that the backhoe was not even invented until 1957. To some of you that may sound like a long time ago. To me, it seems like yesterday.

Even though many of today's jobs didn't exist, the job market seemed endless. Well, almost endless. Television was in its infancy. The picture was black and white, not color. You had only three choices of what to watch; ABC, CBS, or NBC. Cable and Satellite TV did not exist. There were no computers or cell phones, so many of the technical jobs of today didn't exist. Nor did any of the peripheral jobs associated with them.

There were just over 60 in my high school graduating class. The few who went to college knew what they wanted to do. Some wanted to teach, one wanted to be a doctor, and one an engineer.

Only a few of my classmates had parents who could afford to send them to college. Others were smart enough or lucky enough to get scholarships. Some worked part-time paying their own way even though it would take five or six years. It was far different from today, and almost all who went to college knew what they wanted to do in life.

Me, I had no clue what I wanted for a career. So I decided to join the military until I could decide. When I left home to join the U.S. Marine Corps I took all my possessions with me. That consisted of the clothes on my back, the shoes on my feet, and $10 in cash. "Why the Marines, you may ask?" It was because my older brother had joined two years earlier. So, for me it was "Gung Ho" and "Semper Fi" for the next five years.

After five years, I still didn't know what I wanted to do as a career, but I was burned out with the Marines. I was tired of being bossed around, and at the age of 23, I decided to try civilian life. The saying: "The grass always looks greener on the other side of the fence" applied to that choice. What an awakening! I got a short term job as a common laborer, and I discovered that, like in the Marine Corps, I still had a boss telling me what to do.

Shortly before I got out of the Marine Corps in Jacksonville, Florida, I met the love of my life. When I got back home to Perry, I couldn't get her off my mind, so, I went back to Jacksonville and asked her to marry me. Even though I didn't have a job at the time, she said "yes." By this time, more people I knew were going to college.

The GI bill was now available to me, and it could help pay the cost of obtaining a college degree. In addition, if I wanted to go back to school, my fiancée offered to continue working after we were married, but I didn't want her to support me. Plus, I still didn't know what I wanted to do with the rest of my life. So how could I go to college when I didn't even know what to choose for a major?

We got married in 1959, and I went back into the military until I could decide on a career. This time I chose the U.S. Air Force, a less stressful and more-family oriented organization than the Marine Corps. It was a good choice. For the next 18 years I remained in the Air Force, bringing my military career to a total of 23 years. Then I retired at the ripe old age of 41.

I observed that the military seldom rewards

individuality which is not necessarily a bad thing. The military expects cooperation, teamwork, and almost blind obedience to orders. You can advance in the military if you get to work on time, are liked, and get along with everyone, even if you are mediocre.

That is not to say everyone in the military is mediocre. Many, perhaps most are outstanding and competent. However, there were times I had a boss or saw others around me who were mediocre or whose work bordered on incompetence. Sometimes even they would advance because they were well liked and didn't cause any trouble.

Toward the end of my military career, I felt like a cog in a huge machine. I felt as though I was being held back. I wasn't recognized for my abilities or the job I did. Also, because I was enlisted and not an officer, I could never reach my true potential no matter how capable I was. I knew I could never be a Colonel or General. I began to yearn to be recognized and advance based on my work and ability, not my position!

It was when I began to look for a second career that I discovered as a salesman you are judged and paid based on your abilities and the sales you make. It has nothing to do with the time you come to work. It is not how many hours a day you work, even though that can play somewhat of a part. Also, it is not how hard you work unless you are working competently.

An incompetent salesman can work very hard for 10 or 12 hours every day and get nothing in return. The reward is based strictly on what he does during the period of time he works. Therefore, if he wants to succeed, it helps if he becomes competent and knowledgeable as a salesman.

I started preparing myself even before I retired from

the Air Force. I volunteered to become an Air Force recruiter. Someone had told me the Air Force recruiting school was actually a sales school and one of the best in the nation. I found that to be true, as I learned a lot about selling there.

For the next five years, as a recruiter/salesman, I put into practice what I learned. This knowledge and experience would become very beneficial to me when I started my career as a real estate salesman.

Years later, some of the same type individuals who had advanced to a high rank in the military worked for me as real estate salesmen. The ones who studied and learned how to sell succeeded. The others failed. They didn't succeed because they thought all they had to do was, be on time, work hard, get along with others, and be likable.

Those are all good and necessary qualities. However, that is only part of the equation of becoming a successful salesperson. It is also most important and necessary to learn the "how to" of selling. Since they didn't develop that knowledge and those skills, they failed, even though some worked extremely hard. I have seen men and women work very hard, day after day, week after week, and still make no sales.

My ambition was to be financially independent by the time I was 50. As I was starting my second career, I was a long way from that goal which was only nine years away. I realized it would be very difficult to reach such a lofty goal with ordinary income alone. I knew I would have to make wise investments along the way.

I began reading and studying about successful people. **You could do the same!** I discovered that investing was very important. However, one needs money to invest. Therefore, it would be necessary to earn a high income, and you can do it in sales.

A few investors have become successful and wealthy with almost no money. They did it by leveraging. That is extremely risky, and getting wealthy almost never happens that way. Very few people get rich by taking extreme risk. Therefore, because I didn't wish to gamble with my future, I decided to do it the old fashioned way. I decided to learn, work hard, be smart, and invest wisely.

In my research, I discovered something very important. There is no limit to how much a person can earn as a commissioned salesman. I read about Michael Milken. He earned over 500 million dollars in commissions one year by selling junk bonds.

He cut a few unethical and illegal corners along the way and ended up in jail, a totally unnecessary and a stupid thing for him to do, but apparently he got greedy. (Note: I will talk about ethics in selling throughout this book). Even though Michael Milken is an extreme example, I picked him to show there truly is no limit to how much you can earn as a salesman. Can you imagine $500 million dollars earned in one year? (Note: Michael Milken served his time, redeemed himself, and has become an outstanding citizen.)

I chose sales as my second career because my earnings could be unlimited, and I was the sole determining factor. I could have chosen any kind of sales, but I chose real estate because of the many opportunities for investing. You get to know the real estate market and recognize a good investment when you see it. In addition, besides investing in real estate, there are other financial investing opportunities which will be discussed in a future chapter.

Now, let's get started!

# CHAPTER TWO
## Preparing Yourself

I hope your beginning experience will be better than mine. After I had signed all the paperwork for employment as a real estate salesman, the broker/owner turned and walked back into his office and closed the door. I just stood there. Nearby was a large room called a "bullpen" where all the salespeople had their desks.

I wandered around, introduced myself to the salespeople that were in the office, and told them I was going to work there. I asked someone which desks were available. When they told me, I grabbed one and unloaded what little paraphernalia I had and just sat there.

I didn't have any idea of what I should do. So, I started asking questions. I talked to the salespeople, the property manager, the secretary, and anyone else who would listen. I was told which forms were needed to write a listing contract or a sales contract. Then I went out driving around looking for signs in people's yard saying "for sale."

Before long, I actually listed a house. To me, those owner's "for sale" signs were like seeing thousands of dollars lying in people's yard, just waiting for me to come along and scoop them up. What an exciting revelation!

As you start your sales career, always remember that being a salesman is an honorable and important profession. Never think that what you do as a salesman is not important. Believe it or not, the customers need you just as much as you need them.

Here is a short story that will give an example of why a salesman is so important. The year I retired from the military, I took the real estate course, which was required to qualify for getting my license. I was moving to another town, and to get some experience I decided to sell my house on my own without the assistance of a real estate professional.

One day a licensed real estate salesman called me. He said his customer had driven into our neighborhood, saw my "for sale" sign in the yard and liked the looks of the house. The agent asked if he could show it to his customer. I told him he would have to add his commission to my price, which caused the price to go up about $3,000.

The salesman with his customer came out to look at the house. His customer was a Colonel in the Air Force. I thought he was going to buy it; however, I was nervous because the dining room was very small. Sure enough, he said his furniture would not fit in the dining room. That was too bad because he really liked the house.

Later that afternoon, I was riding my bicycle in the neighborhood and noticed another house a little larger than mine, around the corner had just sold that day. Initially, like mine, it wasn't listed with any real estate company. Then I saw the owner's "for sale" sign had been replaced by a real estate company's sign. Atop the sign was a rider showing "SOLD." At the bottom of the sign was the name of the salesman that showed my house.

It turned out the real estate agent had taken the Colonel from my house to the other house, and he bought it. For a long time it puzzled me as to why the Colonel didn't knock on my door or the door of the other house. He was highly educated. Surely he knew he could have saved over $3,000. I really could not understand why!

Later, when I began to sell real estate, I came to understand why he didn't knock on my door. It was because he was moving into a new area and did not know anyone. There were many questions he needed to have answered but didn't know who to ask. His first friend in the area was his real estate agent. The salesman and customer usually develop a bond. It was someone who could answer his questions.

For instance, was the house in a good area? Was it in a good school district? Was it fairly priced? Even when a person is highly educated, that doesn't mean he is educated in all areas.

Maybe there were questions of how to write a contract. It could be that he felt uncomfortable negotiating. Perhaps there were many other questions on his mind. He needed a professional he could trust and rely on to assist him.

Here is a different kind of analogy showing the importance of a professional salesperson. In chemistry class, I discovered a catalyst was a fascinating part of some chemical reactions. Some compounds can be mixed together and nothing happens. You can shake them together, nothing happens. Heat them and still nothing happens.

If you add another compound, a catalyst, the initial compounds will now react with one another. Suddenly there is a chemical reaction. They combine, give off heat, and transform into another compound which is totally different from the original two.

The interesting thing is the catalyst you added doesn't take part in the chemical change. It is not changed in any way. It is not a part of the reaction; it is just sitting there ready to be used again.

Salesmen are like the catalyst. We make things happen without being a part of the transaction, other than being paid for our services. Think about this when you read the story, later in this book, about the buyer and seller both wanting the same drapes. That sale would not have happened without a salesman being involved.

It happens all the time. It is the salesman who makes the difference. So, always remember, and be proud to know that very often you are the most important part of the sale. You are the catalyst!

The one thing you do not have, as a salesman, is the security of an 8 to 5 job. However, there is no job totally secure. You could be laid off or fired. Your company could even go out of business.

Some people cannot work with the stress of not knowing whether they will have a paycheck on a weekly, bi-weekly, or monthly basis. They cannot take that kind of insecurity.

However, always remember that others with average intelligence have succeeded in sales and so can you. To do so, you must have the desire plus confidence in yourself. Like so many things in life, to get ahead, you must take a calculated risk. Notice I said calculated, not "fly by the seat of your pants" type risk.

Only you can evaluate yourself to see if you have the temperament, organizational skill, confidence, motivation, desire, and drive to do what is necessary to succeed as a salesman. The fact that you are reading this book is a strong indication you are on the right track.

As a salesman, you do not have a boss, therefore you have to be your own boss, and you had better be tough on yourself. If you have the traits mentioned above, it is my opinion that you can and will succeed. You will probably obtain goals even higher than you expected.

One of the traits I mentioned above was organizational skills. That is very important. One of the ways to get and stay organized is by using a computer contact program. I will write more about that in another chapter. It is one of the keys to becoming a Super

Salesman.

In preparing yourself, decide early on to be a professional. Look, dress, and sound professional. Learn the terms, the concepts, and all the proper pronunciation you will be using. For instance, you do not sell "real-a-tee", as many sales agents pronounce it. You sell realty. It should be pronounced "real T." I would draw a picture of a "**T**" and ask my new agents, "What do you see?"

If they said it was a "**T**", I would say yes, but more than that, it is a real "**T**." It is a real, honest to goodness drawing of a "**T**." Then I would say, pronounce "realty" as, "real-T." If you join the National Association of REALTORS®, you will become a REALTOR®. That is pronounced "Real tor", not "real-a-tor." Got it?

Another term extremely common in real estate is, "equity." I am amazed at the number of real estate agents who do not know exactly what equity is. Most think they know, but they do not. So, here is the definition.

It is the difference between the amount owed on the property and its selling price. That sounds simple enough, but it isn't. For instance, if someone were to ask you how much equity they have in their home, you can only guess. The true answer will come only when their property sells and closes.

To make sure you understand and to help you remember, I am going to ask you a question. You may think it's a trick question, but it isn't. Do the math, and see if you get the correct answer.

Say you buy a house today for $70,000 and pay $10,000 down payment. You would now owe $60,000, so how much is your equity when you walk out of the closing? Do you think you know? Are you sure? Did you say $10,000? If so, many real estate agents would agree with you. However, I am not going to agree or disagree. I don't know!

If you paid too much for the property and can only sell it for $64,000, even though you paid $10,000 down, your equity is now only $4,000. Again do the math. $64,000 minus the amount owed of $60,000. If you bought it at a steal and could sell it immediately for $79,000, your equity would be $19,000.

Now, it should be very clear. As a real estate salesman or in any other sales profession, there are many terms and concepts you must learn. Learn them so that you will be and sound knowledgeable and professional.

It is not easy to obtain a real estate license. The course is rigorous, and the test is difficult. I believe one of the purposes is to weed out the less qualified and those who will not persevere.

We are protective of our industry and do not want just anyone to get a license. We want to keep the standards high. If you meet these high standards and pass the test; you will get your license and may actually go to work as a salesperson.

Once you have obtained your license and/or a job as a salesman, what do you do? Below, many ideas will be discussed. The idea of a "natural born salesman" is a myth. It may be that selling comes easier for some, but selling is a learned skill.

As difficult as it was to pass the real estate course and license test, you must realize it does not prepare you in any way to be a salesman.

This book is about as close as you will ever come to finding one source of information to teach you everything you need know about selling. Even so, do not limit yourself to this one book.

It will tell you many, if not most of the situations you will encounter and how to handle them. However, there are other great teachers, and for the rest of your selling career you should be a student.

Avail yourself of books, go to seminars, and even brainstorm with other successful salesmen. I hope that does not sound like work because it can be interesting and lots of fun.

You should start preparing yourself personally and financially for selling long before you take the test. The next few paragraphs will list some of the things you could do.

Read good sales and motivational books. A few I can think of are, *How I Raised Myself from Failure to Success in Selling*, by Frank Bettger, *Think and Grow Rich*, by Napoleon Hill, *Psycho Cybernetics*, by Maxwell Maltz, *How to Win Friends and Influence People*, by Dale Carnegie, *The Greatest Salesman in the World*, by Og Mandino. Other authors are Zig Ziglar, Cavett Robert and a whole host of others. You can search for many more authors on the INTERNET.

My favorite is Charlie Cullens. He has a phonograph record that is old and very motivational. I could not find any of his motivational material on the INTERNET. However, if you ever  run across any at a garage sale or old book store, be sure to buy whatever you find.

Another favorite is Frank Bettger. If you are a beginner or an experienced salesman who has become discouraged in selling, you absolutely must read his book, *How I Raised Myself from Failure to Success in Selling*. Reading and studying this book is an absolute must if you want to become a Super Salesman.

Motivational books will excite you, and that is a good thing. However, until you learn the nuts and bolts of selling, what to say, when to say it, and why, it will be like being all dressed up and no place to go. It is the how to of selling that you will learn in this book.

Even though motivational books are important, this book is not written to be motivational. I do hope it will motivate you; however, this is a "how to" book. Unfortunately, there are too few of them. Learn the nuts and bolts of selling, and you **will** succeed.

Next, you must prepare yourself financially. If you sold a house on your very first day, which is unlikely, you wouldn't get a paycheck for at least 30 but more likely 45 days. If you list a house for sale, it may take several months before it sells, and then you must wait another 30 to 45 days until it closes.

There is also a possibility one of your sales will fall through at the last minute before closing. Therefore, under the best of circumstances, you probably will not be getting a paycheck for several months. It will not be good to start out under financial pressure. Therefore, you should have enough money saved up to support yourself and your family for four and preferably six months.

**Always**, after every buyer or seller leaves, you should take a few moments to reflect. In your mind think about everything that was discussed. Think about the questions that were asked and the answers you gave. Think about what was good, what was not so good, and what could have been better. Could you have phrased your question or answer in a more positive or better way? Did you miss an opportunity to ask a closing question?

All this requires **thinking,** and selling is a thinking endeavor. If you miss a sale because you made a mistake or miscalculated, it can be costly. Therefore, you do not want to continually make the same mistakes.

Try to learn something from every customer you encounter. That will help you in later transactions. It is part of the process of learning how to sell by doing and saying things instinctively. Unfortunately most sales agents never learn and keep making the same mistakes time and time again.

**Important lessons in this chapter!**

1. Selling is a very important profession, be proud to be a salesman.

2. Salesmen are like a catalyst, they make things happen.

3. Read books on selling, especially motivational books.

4. Be professional in your dress and knowledge.

5. Always be **listening and thinking** when selling.

6. Evaluate yourself to determine if you have a strong desire, drive, and motivation for a selling career. You do not have a boss, therefore, once you learn what to do, are you disciplined enough to do it?

# CHAPTER THREE
## Preparing the Buyer

Let's start with your very first buyer. You have only your time and abilities to sell. Make sure you use them wisely. Do not get excited just because you have a buyer. You could easily waste a day or two of your time. Make sure the buyer is motivated and financially qualified. Before starting to show houses, it is a good idea to have the buyer pre-qualified by a bank or mortgage company.

If it turns out they are not qualified, let them down gently. Treat them the same way you would a buyer going to buy a million dollar house. Hopefully, you are in this career for the long haul. One day all those potential buyers may be qualified, and you want them to return to you when they can afford to buy. Make them your friend!

Over time, they also may have friends or relatives who want to buy a house. You want them to be a "Center of Influence" for you and send their friends and relatives to you! When they do, you do not have to establish credibility. The fact that you were recommended will mean you already have it.

After you find out your buyers are qualified, find out what their expectations are. You find out by asking questions. Ask them how much they would feel comfortable spending. When you see how much they want to spend, it is up to you to determine if they can afford the house they want for that amount of money.

Again, you do this by asking questions. Ask about the features they would like in their home, do they want a fireplace, number of bedrooms, baths, location, school district, etc. Find out as much as possible.

Often a couple will be surprised to find they are not on the same page with each other in what they want in their home. Each one will have his/her own ideas. It is not unusual for an amateur salesman to show buyers houses all over town. However, he didn't show them any houses on a nearby golf course. That is because the buyers had told him they wouldn't live on a golf course

Later, another salesman sells them a house on the golf course. What happened? What happened is this. What buyers say is only a guide. It may or may not be etched in stone. If what they say is very important, they will let you know.

Show them houses that meet their requirements and desires, even if it is on a golf course. See how they react to it. Even though they may think they know what they want, often they have no clue. Show them the right house, and they will buy it. Talk very little except to ask questions, and listen.

It is the little clues you pick up on that will determine if you should show them the house on the golf course. What I have written here doesn't mean you should constantly show them houses they have said they do not want. Listen and be sensitive to their needs. You may show them one house on the golf course, and see how they react.

Here is an example of how, if you show the right house, it will sell itself. One day I was sitting at my desk showing pictures of houses to my customer. We were getting ready to go look at houses, and I was trying to get an idea of what would suit them. Suddenly the man's eyes lit up, and he exclaimed that he really liked a picture of the house in the booklet.

It was an unusual looking house. He asked how much it cost. When I told him the price, he was very disappointed because the price was more than he wanted to pay. He told me to take it off the list. He felt uncomfortable because of the price; however, it was well within a price range he could afford. Therefore, I left it on the list.

I made it a point to drive by that house. When we got to it, I drove into the driveway. When the man saw it he realized it was the house he had seen in the picture. Very sharply he said to me. "I told you I can't afford this house!" I said, "Yes, I know, but the house is empty, so I want you to look at it, and tell me what you like or don't like about it. It will help me to find you just the right house."

We went inside, and the first thing that jumped out at us was the carpet. I had never seen carpet like that. It was very long black and white shag. It looked like a herd of zebras lying all over the living room. I thought it was a deal breaker, but the carpet made him like the house even more. Suddenly, the man turned to his wife and exclaimed, "Honey, you could get a part-time job."

I smiled because I knew that house was sold. They bought the home and happily lived in it for several years until he was transferred. Remember what I said earlier in this book? Let the house sell itself. Be careful about assuming or making judgments for other people.

Now back to preparing your first buyer. You learn nothing when you are talking. I have been told that a person who talks too much is like a catfish, all mouth and no brains. Many clues come from little side comments. The buyer may talk about their finances, their credit, or lack thereof.

Listen to all the comments they make as you are showing them houses. You may learn something that will be helpful. Make notes that you can refer to later. For example they may talk about a grandparent or an insurance policy, trust fund, etc. If needed, that could be a potential source for raising money for a down payment or help them to qualify for the loan. Remember, never be like a catfish. Always listen to the small talk.

Now, continuing the process and procedure you and the buyer will go through to find and buy a house. This is the procedure you should go through before you start looking.

At this time you can say almost anything without it being stressful. That is because they are not looking at any particular house. No commitments are under consideration. Therefore, this is the time to get all the negative points of buying a house out into the open.

As you get closer to the time of commitment, their stress level will definitely go up considerably. That will not be a good time to bring up anything unexpected, especially if it is negative.

Tell the buyer we will go look at houses. Sometimes I may say house. Other times I may say home. Always be sensitive to what you say and how and when you say it. You should think about the impact your choice of words will have on your customer. For instance, when you start zeroing in on a house they like, it is no longer a house. It is important to call it a **home**. That brings the emotion into the sale.

Tell the buyer after we find the **home** they like, "We will all return to the office and fill out the paperwork. At that point, tell them it is called an offer because they are offering to buy the home.

Even if the offer is exactly the seller's asking price, it is called an offer until both the buyer and seller sign. Then it becomes a contract. Instead of saying contract, I usually call it an "agreement;" the word contract seems to make people nervous. The offer will list the price, terms of the sale, the date of occupancy, and other stipulations.

You should get out the blank offer forms, and go over all the details. Let them see, touch, and get very familiar with the forms. That way, it will not be intimidating when you pull out the forms at the time of signing. You tell them when an offer is made that it is a common practice to put up Earnest Money. Make sure you are very clear, and they understand everything about the Earnest Money.

Earnest Money is normally a check, and it is not cashed **unless** the offer is accepted. Make sure they understand if the offer is accepted, their check **will be cashed**. Early in my career, a buyer's check bounced, and they got very upset. That was because all they heard was their check wouldn't be cashed. They didn't hear "unless the offer is accepted." Make sure they understand their check will be cashed and held in trust if their offer is accepted by both buyer and seller.

You then tell the buyer, based on the price range of the house, what a reasonable amount for Earnest Money should be. You determine the amount based on your judgment. I always got almost double the amount of other sales agents in my company.

I learned early in my career, the more Earnest Money you get the more likely the sale will close. If the buyer objects and thinks it is too much; discuss it. Maybe they know someone who put up less money. Tell them the amount is negotiable and can be less.

However, if they are buying a house and making a low offer, tell them a larger amount of Earnest Money will make them appear to be a better, more qualified, and serious buyer. Thus, the seller will be more inclined to accept their low offer. Remind them the Earnest Money is held in "trust" and comes back to them at closing.

I would sometimes say it is like taking money out of one pocket and putting it into another. Tell them it can be used as the down payment or closing cost, etc. Get as much as possible. **You get more by asking for more!** I learned that lesson from the Bible. It says, "Ask, and it shall be given you."

You tell your buyers if everything is acceptable to the seller and they sign your offer, you have a contract or agreement. On the other hand, if the seller doesn't accept and changes any term of your offer, it comes back to you as a counteroffer. At that point, it is up to you to accept, reject, or even make a counteroffer to the seller's counteroffer.

At the time the offer is finally accepted and signed by both parties, it becomes a contract. That is called "a meeting of the minds." Then their Earnest Money check **will be cashed** and held in trust until closing.

Ask your buyers if they have the Earnest Money available right now. They may not have any money at all. They may be planning to borrow it, which could cause them to not qualify for the home loan. Even though they think they have money, it may not be available until sometime in the future.

It could be Certificates of Deposit maturing or a payoff from an insurance claim, it may be an income tax refund or money from a trust fund, it could be a gift from a parent or grandparent, etc. You need to know all this. It could be that your buyer is not financially capable of buying at this time. If so, you want to find out before you waste your time and gas showing them houses all over town.

So far, there should be little if any stress, as they are not making any kind of decision or commitment. You are simply explaining the procedure. Because of that, they are much more relaxed and likely to give you the information you want and need.

Those same questions could be very stressful at the time of commitment, the time they are about to sign the offer. At that time, they are deciding about buying a particular home. They may be afraid, unsure, and extremely nervous. You do not want any other issues to surface. The worst possible time to talk about Earnest

Money is at the signing of the Offer.

Many and probably most salesmen wait until the signing of the offer to tell the buyers about the Earnest Money. That should not be a problem for you because you have already explained it. It is one of the main purposes of going over the procedure before leaving the office to look at houses.

When it comes time to sign the offer, your buyers will know what is expected, so just write up the offer. Do not ask anything about the Earnest Money. Simply write down the amount you discussed earlier. **Note:** After the Offer is signed, do not forget to get the Earnest Money, whether it is a check or promissory note. I will discuss promissory notes later in this chapter.

Before you present the written offer for signature, tell your buyers they can read it if they wish. But because there is a lot of legal jargon in it, you would like to make sure they understand everything. Then go through every paragraph one by one. Don't read it; just give a brief explanation of what it says. You should also tell them to ask any questions they may have.

This is a procedure you should use when you are ready for the buyer to sign the contract. After you have answered their questions, give them the pen, and ask for their OK on the bottom line. Note; I **didn't say sign** the offer or contract. It is a lot less stressful or frightening to OK something than it is to sign a contract.

Do this **exact same procedure** with every buyer at the signing of the offer or contract. Later, if there is a misunderstanding, it will be easier for you to remember, and restructure everything that happened at the time of signing. You will know because you do it exactly the same way every time with every customer.

Later, if a problem or misunderstanding arises, remind your customer that you told them they could read the contract and ask questions if they wish. Tell them to remember how you explained it, paragraph by paragraph, and asked if they understood or had any questions. By doing it that way, there should seldom, if ever, be a problem because of a misunderstanding.

It could happen that you have a buyer who is lacking integrity. It may be that he changed his mind for some reason and wants to get out of the contract. If he doesn't want to take the blame, he may fabricate events to make it look like it was someone else's fault.

It will be much easier to recall anything that happened out of the ordinary if you do it exactly the same way every time with all your customers. Later, if a problem arises, believe me; you will be glad you always do it the same way.

This brings up another point concerning "Errors and Omission" insurance. Without elaborating, I highly recommend you have it. The more business you do, the more you will need it. We live in a litigious society. Often if you are sued you will win; however, the cost of defending yourself is outrageous. The National Association of REALTORS® or your state association has insurance available for a reasonable price.

Suppose after signing the Offer, the buyer says, "Oops, I left my checkbook at home, or My Certificate of Deposit doesn't mature until next Tuesday." That means they have no money for the Earnest Money. That could be a deal killer. That is, unless you are prepared. In sales, **never,** put off until tomorrow what can be done today. Remember the saying, "Tomorrow never comes." Always think of a way you can get the contract signed **now** instead of later. Remember, another offer could come in while they are on the way home to get their check book.

Have blank listing and sales contract forms with you at all times. I almost want to say even in the shower. You also should have any other forms that you may need in a sales transaction, including blank promissory notes. That will help you to avoid any type of delay. I have seen sales lost because of a short delay of less than an hour. Explain to the buyer that they can sign a note, and then bring the money or check at whatever time you will have established.

After the offer and promissory note are signed **and not before**, you need to explain that the note is just like they had given you the check they had forgotten. You should explain that the note is like handing you a check or cash, and it can be collected in a court of law. Above I placed "and not before" in bold letters. That is to emphasize to you not to scare them when they are about to sign.

Don't let them leave thinking they can change their mind simply because they only gave you a promissory note. The reason is once the contract is signed often the buyer begins to worry. They may even change their mind about buying the house. We in the industry call it "Buyer's Remorse."

I encountered it so often that I got some small clear plastic pill containers and placed M&Ms in them. I sorted the M&Ms so that each container would have the same color. Some containers had brown, some green, some yellow, etc. It was just like any other container of pills. I labeled them as follows:

NERVE PILLS (Do not swallow, CHEW ONLY)
- Better Deal Syndrome: Take 2 pills and chew
- Did I pay too much? Take 2 pills and chew
- Want to think about it: Take 3 pills and chew
- General Buyers Nervousness: Take 1 pill and chew

I told the buyer to expect those feelings as most people have them. It was my way of saying this is normal and to expect it. I would say take your pills, chew, and you will feel better in the morning. We would all have a laugh.

This was very effective in lessening the stress. If later, they were still worried about something, we would discuss it. If it turned out to be insignificant, as often it was, I would tell them to take an extra nerve pill. We would have a laugh, and usually that would be the end of it.

## Important lessons in this chapter!

1.  Do not waste your time with non-qualified buyers. Make sure they are motivated, capable financially, and their expectations are in line with what they can afford.
2.  Do more Listening than talking. Don't be like a catfish, all mouth & no brains.
3.  Up front, go through the procedure of buying before there is the stress of making a decision.
4.  Explain the procedure about Earnest Money. Find out if it is available now, where it is coming from, and get as much as is reasonably possible.
5.  In writing the offer, assume the earnest money is the amount discussed earlier, and place it on the offer form without asking permission.
6.  Have the forms needed for listing and selling with you at all times so that you are always ready for business.
7.  Always use the exact same procedure before signing an offer or contract. That will make it easier to reconstruct or discuss later if the need arises.

# CHAPTER FOUR
## Finding a Home For the Buyer

Even though this is your first buyer, the concepts you will learn in this chapter, and those learned in the previous chapter apply to all buyers. That means every buyer should be treated like your first buyer.

When you go to show houses to your customers, the seating arrangement in the car is extremely important. Sometimes a couple may have jealousy issues. If you are a male sales agent, always tell the woman you will be her chauffeur for the day, and open the back car door for her.

If you are a female sales agent, it is very important to place the woman in the front and the man in the back seat. Of course, if one of them says they would rather sit in the front or back, let them sit where they want.

As you are showing houses, do not ignore one of the parties. If you have a couple, talk to both of them. Get them both equally involved. It may be that one is easier to talk to than the other. If you favor that person, you could have a hostile situation and not even know it.

You never know who will make the final decision to buy. Therefore, if you favor one over the other, you could very likely lose the sale. If you are a male salesman, never talk down to a female customer. The same applies if you are a female and your customer is a male. Treat everyone as an equal.

Before heading out to look at houses, you need to pick several houses to view. Time is important, and gas is expensive. Therefore, map out your route. Most times, as a general rule you will want to pick the most direct route without backtracking. However, you can make exceptions to this rule.

For example, after you have gained experience, there will be times you will feel instinctively that you know which house the buyer will buy. When you have that feeling, do not go directly to that house. You may want to stage the showing by going through that area, and then show them houses in another area. That way, the buyers can begin to get a feel for different areas as well as houses.

When they get to the house you have in mind; they will have seen other areas and houses to compare. It is uncanny to me, how buyers will get a feel for areas and values as they look at houses. Also, it is not a good idea to show houses that are much nicer and more expensive than the house they will probably buy. That may increase their desire for a home they cannot afford.

As you approach the house you think they are going to buy, do not start selling them on how wonderful it is. For instance, if they want a pool, and you know it has a gorgeous pool, don't tell them about it; let them walk up on it. It will be much more exciting for them. You could even tag along behind as they wander through the house and discover its features by themselves.

After they have seen the house, you can discuss what they like or do not like about it. Based on what they say, you may want to paint a picture of them in it. For instance, you might ask where would they place their couch or how would they set up the dining room, bedrooms, etc. That brings emotion into the sale.

In all cases do not try to sell the merits of any house before they see it. If you oversell, it could be a let down when they view it. Let the features and quality of the house sell itself. It is always best to let buyers discover the features of a house. Of course, if they overlook something, you could point it out to them.

As you are walking up the walkway to the house, the

buyer may ask, "Does it have a fireplace?" You know it has the most magnificent fireplace in town. How do you answer? I will discuss these kinds of questions in Chapter Ten titled: *Asking and Answering Questions*. Rather than have you jump ahead, I will tell you how to answer that question now.

Many sales people will tell the buyer how wonderful and magnificent the fireplace is. The buyer may then say they hate fireplaces, they are nasty and stink. They do not want to look at the house because they wouldn't live in a home with a fireplace.

That agent may have dug himself a deep hole, and he may not be able to get out of it for that house. The best answer is, "Do you want a fireplace?" If they say "yes", even though you know it has a fireplace, you may say, "Let's look and see." It's always best to let them discover it. If they say no, they hate fireplaces, here is what you say.

But first let me digress for a moment. Before you answer their question, find out how important it is to them. For example ask, "Do you want a fireplace?" It may or may not be important at all. Do not try to sell a feature in which the buyer has no interest.

Any question asked by a customer that may have a negative answer must be answered immediately, "yes," "no," "I don't know," or any other answer that is honest and appropriate. Only after you have answered their question should you attempt to sell them on that negative feature.

Now back to the above question. The buyer just told you he hates fireplaces because they are nasty and stink. Therefore, he wouldn't buy a house with a fireplace. You have a problem because this may be the very house you were sure he was going to buy. So, here is how you could answer. "Yes, this house has a fireplace, but let me hasten to say, you don't have to use it as a fireplace. You could clean it out and place candles in it. That could make it a great focal point for the room."

You could say, "Place gas logs in it that crackle and pop just like a fireplace burning logs. Then if you ever decide to sell the house, the fireplace will be a great selling feature." You notice that I answered "yes" immediately before going on, to sell it as a positive feature.

Part of selling is thinking on your feet. Notice also, in this instance, I didn't let them discover the fireplace. I prepared them in advance. Since it is a negative for them, I immediately started selling them on the idea of falling in love with a fireplace even though they said they hate them. Don't be surprised if they change their mind and buy the house.

Another question a buyer may ask is, "Does it have a large yard?" Reply by asking, "Do you want a large yard?" Obviously you cannot change the size of the yard. But keep in mind that size is relative. Large to one person may be small to another. It may be that all yards in that neighborhood are large.

If the buyer says he doesn't want a large yard, you can answer; "It is about average for this neighborhood." There is no need to elaborate. The question may never come up again. But if it is important to him, he will let you know. Sometimes when you ask if it is important, he will say. "No, I was just curious."

Keep in mind that many questions you may be asked are not important at all, that is, unless you make it important. Sometimes it's just the buyer making small talk. If it's important, the buyer will definitely let you know. Many times if you ignore a question, it will never come up again. Even so, remember to always listen while participating in small talk. You never know when a closing question may be asked.

When showing houses your ultimate goal is to find your buyers the house they want as quickly as possible. You want to be sociable without socializing. Ask questions, then listen, and think as they answer your questions. Listen for clues to find out what the buyers think of the house at which they are looking. Especially listen for a **closing** question.

You will be given more information on closing questions in Chapter Ten. Your closing question may be something like this. The buyer asks, "Will the refrigerator stay?" Your reply is, "Do you need or want a refrigerator?" If they say, "Yes", then ask if they would be interested in this house if the refrigerator remained.

If they answer "yes" to that question, they have just told you they would possibly buy that house. Therefore, you say, "We can go back to the office and put it on paper and see what the seller says." That is better than saying "make an offer." You did it without asking them to buy or sign anything. Can you see how much easier it will be for the buyer to be in agreement?

**Never** ask for a signature unless you have the documents before them, and they are ready to be signed. Even then, you ask them to put their OK on the bottom line, rather than "sign here." If the house is vacant or if no one is home, you could sit down right there, and do the paperwork without going back to the office. Again I reiterate, remember to always have fill in the blank offer/contract forms with you at all times.

Selling is all about closing, and the big closing comes at the end of the sale. For many salespeople it is dreaded. Even I dreaded the closing when I was an amateur salesman but not anymore.

The closing is dreaded because that is when you get

the rejection. However, every closing question leads you to the big and final closing question and signature. If you set the stage and handle it correctly, closing will be the most fun and exciting part of the sale. You will look forward to it.

The sale should be broken down into many closing questions spread throughout the sale. For instance, if the buying vibes are there, you may ask, "When would you like to move in?" That is a strong closing question. Just wait for the answer, even if it takes five minutes. The buyer may shock you and say next week, or I am not sure I want this house.

At least now, you know more about what the buyer is thinking. Isn't this fun? I just re-read this chapter. There is a lot of good stuff in it. It is getting me excited just thinking about some of my past closings. Selling is all about closing. It can be exciting and great fun if handled correctly. It also can be the most difficult part of the sale if handled poorly. Go back and re-read this chapter, and think as you are reading it!

## Important lessons in the chapter!

1. Pay attention to the seating arrangement of your customers when they get into your car.

2. In your conversation, don't favor one over the other. Never talk down to your customer, especially if they are of the opposite sex. Treat all customers as an equal.

3. Remember to find out what the customer wants before answering their question. You don't want to sell them on something in which they have no interest.

# CHAPTER FIVE
## Thinking While Selling

As discussed earlier, thinking is a very important part of selling. The interests of the buyer and seller are often diametrically opposed to one another. Therefore, in addition to thinking about what you are going to say, you must also think about whether you are talking to the buyer or the seller. The buyer wants to spend as little as possible, and the seller wants to get as much as possible.

So, think about who you are talking to at the moment. For instance, if you are talking to a buyer, you may phrase your comment differently than if you make a similar comment to the seller. I am not talking about being dishonest. Just do not unnecessarily emphasize a negative point. That is why you must be thinking at all times.

A good example is in Chapter Ten when I called the seller's drapes "old" and "used." Even though I said it to the seller, I would never make a comment like that to the buyer.

Buyers and sellers are different and must be treated differently. Here is an example of why and what you must be thinking according to whether you are talking to the buyer or seller. In pricing a house, I suggest you use a technique retail marketers use.

If you go into any retail store, you will notice few items sell for a whole dollar amount. For example, an item may be priced at $9.98, not $10. The retailer wants the customer to think $9 range, not $10. They know the price is more appealing to buyers if it is just under the whole dollar amount.

As you read the next paragraph, slow down, and think as you read. Think as you shift back and forth to each side of the transaction.

Use the same method that retailers use when pricing a property. When you are dealing with a seller, he may want to list his house for $70,000. Try to get the seller to round his price down, asking $100 **less,** to $69,900. In this example, the potential buyer will be thinking $60,000 price range, instead of $70,000.

On the other hand, if a house is on the market for $72,900 and a buyer wants to make a low offer of $69,900. Tell him to offer $100 **more**. A price of $70,000 will be much more appealing to the seller. He will be happy that he didn't sell in the $60s range. Therefore, he is more likely to accept that low offer. Always try to get the buyers to **round up** and the sellers to **round down**. To do this you have to think of which side of the transaction you are working.

Sometimes you may talk to both buyer and seller in the same transaction. Since they are on different sides of the transaction, you have to be aware of which one you are talking to. This is far from being dishonest. It is simply being sensitive to the needs and desires of the person to whom you are talking. Again, remember you are the catalyst, bringing together a meeting of the minds between two parties with opposing interest.

The next chapter will be on listening. I once read that we should listen more than we talk. Since we have two ears and only one mouth, it makes sense that we should listen more than we talk. In this book, every time you see the word **think**, remember the word **listen**. You listen to learn, not to reply! Often you have to listen to know what you should be thinking. In every phase of the sale you may have opportunities provided you don't miss them. That is why you must always be listening and thinking.

You should think about how you will phrase a

question. Think about how you will answer a question. People do not like problems, therefore, never have one. Instead, say we have a situation, and here are your options. Think about how the person you are talking to may feel about what is happening at the moment. Think about how a buyer or seller may feel. Think about how a non-qualified buyer may feel when he finds out he doesn't qualify for a loan.

While selling, you must be listening and thinking from beginning to end. If this is not natural for you, you must consciously work on it. I will not expound on this subject any further in this chapter. However, throughout the book, I will point out situations explaining why and what you should be thinking.

I will sometimes put the word listen or think in bold letters. That is to keep reminding you to be constantly listening and thinking. **Think, think, think**, and then think some more. Read this chapter again slowly. Pause after each paragraph, and reflect on what you have just read. Let it soak in until it becomes a part of how you think. There is a lot of powerful information here.

## Important lessons in this chapter!

1. You must be constantly aware to really **think** and **listen** when you are with your customers. Listen to **learn,** not to **respond**.

2. You should reflect and analyze to learn something from every customer and situation in which you are involved.

# CHAPTER SIX

## Listening

In the previous chapter I said, "Every time you see the word think, remember the word listen." However, because listening is **SO** important, this chapter will deal with this most important part of selling.

There is no gift you can give that will impress anyone as much as listening, really listening. You may think a gift such as an automobile or a diamond ring will do the trick. Yes, it will be impressive but only for a fleeting moment. Even that will not compete with the art of listening.

Whether it is matters of the heart, developing a friendship, or making a sale, nothing is more powerful than listening. When I was courting my wife, we would sit on the front stoop talking for hours and listening to one another. Now she says I never listen. Oh well, that's another story.

I remember a story my father told me when I was a young boy. I will not quote him; I will just tell the story as I recall it. He said, when he married my mother, he had very little formal education. He made a living by delivering papers for *The Tampa Morning Tribune*. His boss, Jim was called a road man, which is like an area manager. That job was only slightly more important than my father's.

As time passed, my father quit delivering papers and became a barber. Years later he was talking with someone, and they mentioned that his old boss was now the publisher of *The Tampa Morning Tribune*.

My father could not believe he had risen to such a lofty position in the company, and he decided to go by and visit him the next time he was in Tampa, Florida.

When he went to Jim's office, the secretary said he was very busy, but maybe they could speak to one another briefly. When Jim came out of his office to greet my father, he also said he was very busy and could only talk with him for a very few minutes.

As they were talking, my father asked how he had gone from being a road man to being the top man in the company. Three hours later when they emerged from his office, Jim told my father how much he really enjoyed the conversation and to please come back anytime.

Dad said he hardly spoke a word. He just sat and listened with a nod and a comment every now and then. On the other hand, Jim was having the time of his life as he reminisced by telling how he rose through the corporate ranks to the top position in the company. If my father had been a salesman, he could have sold Jim anything that day.

How many times have you been talking and noticed the person you were talking to was not listening? If that happens, just stop talking. You may be surprised that often the person will not realize you have stopped. If he hasn't forgotten it altogether, several minutes later he may say; "Oh, what were you saying?"

You should always be a good listener, but it works both ways. Make sure your customers are listening when you are talking. Watch their facial expressions, and be alert to their reactions. If they are not listening, it makes no sense to continue because they will not hear what you say.

Perhaps it would be better if you stopped talking and encouraged the other person to talk so you can find out what is on his mind. All good salesmen are good listeners. To become a Super Salesman, it is imperative that you learn, develop, and practice the art of being a good listener.

People are much more interested in what they have to say than in what you have to say. Therefore, let them say it. If you do, they will be much more likely to listen to you and buy your product.

One of the most important reasons for listening is to establish rapport and friendship. Another reason is to learn. By listening, you can find out what the other person wants. Selling then becomes a matter of helping them find a way to get it.

This is a chapter that you should review often. Refer back to it until you become a good listener without even thinking about it.

**Important lessons in this chapter!** Make listening a habit; listen to make friends as well as customers. Remember, you listen to learn not to respond.

# CHAPTER SEVEN

## Farming

Does it seem odd that I would have a chapter on Farming? I am not talking about tilling the soil or selling farms; I am talking about building a real estate prospect farm. It is an excellent way to start out as a real estate salesman. I will tell you my experience.

When I retired from the U.S. Air Force, I moved to a small town in South Georgia. Since I knew only about three people in the town, I had no one to ask for referrals. About that time, I read a pamphlet on building a real estate prospect farm. It told me a few of the things I would need to do. So, I decided to make my real estate prospect farm the subdivision where I lived. After all, I was there a considerable amount of time.

It was a fairly new subdivision and had about 100 houses and growing. The first thing I did was to get a plat of the subdivision which had every lot listed. I tacked it on the back of my bedroom door. Next, I started walking or riding my bicycle throughout the neighborhood. I knocked on every door and introduced myself.

I told the occupants I was their new neighbor, and I was going into the business of selling real estate. I told them if they ever had a question about real estate to call me at any time, day or night. Even on weekends, I would take their call.

I told them if they thought their taxes were too high I would tell them how to challenge the assessment. I would even go to the courthouse with them and show them how; some took me up on it. I had a notepad with me and wrote down their names, phone numbers, the names of their children, their ages, and even the dog's name if they had one. I don't remember getting any cat's names. Also, if possible, I would get birthdates, so I could send them birthday cards. When I went home, I wrote the information in pencil on the plat on the back of my bedroom door.

As I was making my rounds, I went to a neighbor's house that had a real estate lockbox on it. There was no sign in the yard, so I asked him why the lock box was on his door. He told me his house had been on the market to sell, but it didn't sell. He said the real estate salesman picked up his sign but had forgotten to get his lock box. I asked if he still wanted to sell. He said, "Yes." So, I relisted it on the spot. By the time I had finished meeting every neighbor, I had three listings.

Every time a house sold in my neighborhood farm, I would send a card or letter to everyone, telling them the address of the house that had sold. If I could get permission from the new buyer, I would write in my letter or card telling the name and occupation of the person soon to be their new neighbor. Also, I would go by and wish my departing neighbor good luck and told them I hoped they would enjoy their new location.

I would ask if they were talking with a real estate agent in the location where they were moving. If they were not, I would try to get permission to contact an agent for them. That way I would get a referral fee. When I went home, I would erase the name of the old neighbor and add the name of the new one.

As time went on, I began to get more and more of the listings in my neighborhood farm. Hardly a week went by that I didn't have something to report. Maybe it was a new listing or sale of a house or anything else of interest.

I was constantly sending out cards and letters reminding my neighbors if they had any real estate needs to call me, I was just moments away. I was always knocking on doors or stopping to chat when I would see anyone out in their yard. Hopefully I was not too much of a pest. Then a couple of interesting things happened.

At our monthly local Board luncheon, I overheard two real estate agents talking to one another. One mentioned that he saw a "For Sale by Owner" (FSBO) sign in my neighborhood.

The other agent told him not to waste his time. He said, "Hoot has pretty much sewed up that subdivision. He will probably get that listing." He told the other agent his time would be better used in a different area. Now that is powerful when you get that kind of reputation with your competitor sales agents.

Another interesting thing happened about that time. One day I saw a neighbor who lived several houses down from me come into my office. All our sales agents worked in a large office that we called a Bullpen. We would often see and know with whom other agents were working.

This neighbor, an insurance salesman, went to lunch with one of my fellow sales agents. She was a client of his. When they returned from lunch, she came up to me with a handful of letters and cards and plopped them down on my desk.

She said my neighbor gave them to her saying, "If I get any more letters or cards from Hoot, I think I'll scream." She took great delight in delivering that message to me. As in many industries, sometimes there is professional jealousy.

Paul Harvey, the famous newscaster, often said; "Now for the rest of the story." It is almost unbelievable, but about a week later, that same neighbor called me. I was at home having lunch. He wanted to know if I could come by and see him, like right now. It sounded as though he was in a panic.

I walked down the street to his house. He told me he had just found out he was being transferred out of state.

He said he was leaving at the end of the week, and his family was staying behind until their house sold. Therefore, he needed to sell immediately. Of course, I listed the house right then.

Our office had a policy on relations with our fellow sales agents. We were not allowed to interfere or try to take customers from one another. The only exception was if, without any encouragement on your part, the customer specifically asked for you. So, I waited. I knew I would be contacted shortly by the other agent. Sure enough when she saw the listing, she came storming over and wanted to know how I got that listing.

A week earlier, that agent had gotten great delight in telling me my neighbor wanted to scream as she plopped down the cards and letters on my desk. It probably gave me just as much satisfaction when I told her I was very surprised when he called and asked me to come over and list his house.

It did puzzle me as to why he didn't list with the sales agent he took to lunch since she had bought an insurance policy from him, and she was his client. As I always do, I analyze and think so I can learn from each customer. Here is my conclusion. I believe my neighbor did in fact give those letters and cards to my fellow sales agent.

I believe he was sincere when he said he wanted to scream. However, he did not have a need at the time. Shortly afterward, when he did have a need, he called me. It was because he knew I was the one making things happen, by selling the majority of houses that were sold, in our neighborhood. Isn't that interesting?

**An important lesson in this chapter!** Become well known in your real estate prospect farming area. Become known as the "go to" person for listing and selling houses.

# CHAPTER EIGHT
## The Importance Of Listing

A good salesman gets what he wants by helping others get what they want. You do not always have to have a tangible product to sell. You can sell an idea or concept. If you are trying to get an appointment, you are actually selling for the appointment; it is intangible but a sale nonetheless.

When you get the appointment, you just made a sale. If it is a listing you are after, you may have to make several sales before you make the final sale of getting the listing. The first sale may be just getting the prospect to talk to you. Next is getting the appointment. It is at the appointment that you attempt to make the final sale of getting the listing.

Before the federal "No Call" list, you could pick up your phone and call a potential seller. Now, you may have to get your leads by mailing letters, knocking on doors, Centers of Influence (more on that later), setting up a booth or kiosk, an expired listing in the Multi-List System, advertising in the newspaper, radio, television, or INTERNET, etc. Even though some things have changed and are continuing to change since I was actively selling, the concepts remain the same.

Today, people are bombarded with sales ads on TV, radio, newspaper, magazines, INTERNET, mail, email, and even people who call, constantly violating the "No Call" list. Few people will ever want to talk to you about listing their home. Therefore, talk about selling, not listing, their home. Get the words "list" or "listing" out of your vocabulary when talking to potential sellers. As a salesman, few people if any want to talk to you at all; that is unless you say something that gets their attention and makes them want to talk to you.

That being the case, you must think of reasons to make them want to talk to you. For instance, you may say you have some ideas that will help them sell their home. That statement may cause them to want to make an appointment.

**Think**! You can always come up with some good ideas. Follow up with a closing question like, "When can we get together to discuss these ideas?" Most sellers will want to know what your ideas are. Make sure you **do** have something to tell them. You have just asked a closing question, and you are trying to close for an appointment.

Actually, you are in the process of making two sales. First is the appointment, the listing sale comes later. Be sure to keep it in that order. Remember, at this point you are not trying to list their house. You are trying to make an appointment. The listing is a different sale and comes during the appointment. It is totally separate.

To list the house, you need to be in front of the seller with the proper paperwork to sign. Never try to list a house or sell anything over the phone. Even if you are successful, they may cool down and change their mind by the time you get to them with the listing forms. If you are talking to them on the phone, try only to get the appointment.

Sellers will probably ask what your ideas are. Give them one idea as a teaser. Immediately follow up by asking for the appointment. Do not let them pull all your ideas from you. If you do, there is no need for them to make the appointment because you would have nothing new to tell them. After telling them you have some ideas, ask when would be a good time to get together to discuss these ideas.

You can give them several reasons for the appointment. For instance, you could say that you would like to see their home. If you have already seen it, say you would like to re-familiarize yourself with it. Give them an alternative option, say "Would 2 p.m. be OK or would 7 p.m. be better?" They may answer, "how about tomorrow at 4 p.m.?" That is called giving an "alternative of choices."

Remember what to do each time you ask the closing question. If you are in their presence smile, look them in the eyes, and wait for their answer. If you are on the phone, just be silent, and wait for their answer.

Here are some examples of "alternative of choices" type questions. If you are selling cars, you could ask, "Would you rather have the red car or the blue one?" If selling suits, it could be, "Would you consider the sports coat or do you want something dressier?" For houses, you might say, "Would you like to move in this week or would next week be better?" This technique can be used in many selling situations. Think and build a large repertoire of "alternative of choices" type questions to ask in various situations.

It is my opinion that listing properties is perhaps more important than selling properties. There are several reasons for this. One reason is buyers are not so easily found. When you list properties, you can make things happen. Sellers are everywhere, and they are easy to find. Many times they even put a sign in their yard telling you they are a seller. Yes, it is easy to find sellers. You know they are everywhere because you see their advertisements.

Just look in the newspaper or the INTERNET. Take a ride around town, and look for signs in people's yard. You can go into a neighborhood, and knock on doors, and ask if they have an interest in selling their home. Even if they don't, they may know of someone down the street or across town that does.

When you list a property and place it into the Multi-List system, you can move on to something else. You now potentially have every real estate sales agent in town working for you. They will try to sell your listings. That's a good deal. They are working for you, and you don't even have to pay them unless they actually make the sale.

After listing a property and placing a sign in the seller's yard, it should have a rider on top with your name and cell phone number on it. That makes it an advertisement specifically for you. If a potential buyer comes along and likes the looks of the property, chances are he will call you.

Even though he may not buy the house he called on, you now have a potential buyer for one of the other houses you have listed. The more properties you have listed, the more signs you will have with your name and phone number all over town. Thus, more potential buyers will be contacting you.

The more control you have of the inventory of properties for sale, the more buyers will be coming to you. Also, all the other sales agents will be working for you through the Multi-List system.

Another advantage of carrying a large inventory of properties to sell is this; when you have a buyer, there is a good chance somewhere in your inventory you may have a property for that buyer. Therefore, you will not have to split a commission with another sales agent. That is unless you work in a state or company that only allows you to work with the buyer or seller but not both. In that case, you may be able to refer that customer to another agent and get a referral fee.

Now let's talk about finding buyers. If your boss said to you, "Go find a buyer today." What would you do?

Buyers are not like sellers. You won't find their advertisement in the newspaper, the INTERNET, or a sign in their yard.

Where would you go to find a buyer? Can you see how that could be much more difficult than finding a seller? If you concentrate your efforts on buyers only, you have to wait for the buyer to contact you. In my opinion, that makes you less of a salesman and more of an order-taker.

You may be a good or even a great salesman after you get the buyer. You may even make a comfortable living. However, to be a Super Salesman, you must make things happen! If possible you should work with both sellers and buyers.

On the other hand, if your boss said, "Go find a seller." You would know where to go. They are definitely out there, and they are easily found. Check ads in the newspaper. Ride around town looking for a "For Sale" sign in an owner's yard. Ask your friends or prior customers. Knock on doors. If you look, you can easily find them.

You need to know that there is a downside to listing properties. As soon as you list the property, the seller expects you to sell it almost immediately. That can cause you a lot of emotional stress. Think about it. If you have 30, 40, 50, or more properties listed and they don't sell quickly, that can mean a lot of irate sellers. They will call you day and night. That is especially true if you do not stay in touch with them.

Many sales agents avoid the seller after listing their property. That's because they know, if it doesn't sell right away, the seller doesn't mind letting you know they are upset.

It means you could have a big problem if you carry a real large inventory of properties to sell. That being the case, you must educate your sellers. Let them know that under the best of circumstances, it could take three or more months on average to sell a house in their area. Tell them you will call at least once a week, and give a report, even if nothing is happening. That way they will know you are still on the job.

Tell your sellers you have a large inventory of listings. Then, hasten to tell them that is a good thing. Otherwise, they may think you are off trying to sell your other listings, instead of theirs. Let them know it is good to have many listings because the more houses you have listed, the more buyers will be calling.

Tell them someone may call from a sign they saw in another part of town. After finding out the particulars about the house they called on, they may not be interested in it. However, your seller's house may be the exact one for them, and they may buy it. Explain it that way to all the sellers whose houses you have listed.

Let the sellers know they also can help in the sale of their home. Tell them you will be working as a team. Usually, I would tell them if a potential buyer drives by and if they or anyone else asks about their home don't send them to me! That always shocked them; I said it to get their attention.

Then I would explain it like this. I would tell them it may be that the potential buyer has phone numbers from signs on other houses they have seen. If they call one of those numbers, there is a chance another sales agent will get involved, and you may never see or hear from that buyer again.

I tell the seller, if you give the potential buyer my phone number, the buyer may not call it. Therefore, the seller needs to get the name and phone number of the potential buyer. I emphasize that even though they give my number to the buyer, they should not depend on him to get in touch with me. Tell the seller he needs to call me. Really emphasize that to your sellers, otherwise they may not do it. Better yet, I always told my sellers to try to get in contact with me, if possible, while the potential buyer is still with them.

Let the seller know you will hunt down those potential buyers. However, to do so, you will need as much information about them as possible. Therefore, they should get their name, phone number, and where they are staying. If they are in a motel, get the name of the motel, their room number, as well as the phone number of the motel.

Another thing you could emphasize to the seller is for them to always keep the conversation positive when you call to give them an update on the selling activity of their home. Tell them if they have suggestions or complaints, you want to hear them. However, let them know you don't only want to hear complaints every time you call just because the house hasn't sold.

Remind them that you will be calling many other sellers. Tell them it can be very depressing to listen to everyone complain. After several hours of listening to those complaints, it can be so depressing it may make you want to go home and crawl into a little ball. Tell them you have to work hard at staying motivated in order to be able to work effectively at selling their property.

If you prepare and educate your sellers properly, it will be much easier for you to stay in touch with them. Later when you move from the ranks of being a great salesman to becoming a Super Salesman, you will not have time to make all those calls personally; your assistant will be making some of them for you. Let your sellers know that the assistant is calling on your behalf so you can use your time more productively in selling their home. This will be discussed more in the last chapter.

Now that you have set the stage, for goodness sake, **stay in touch**! When you call your sellers and get an answering machine, always leave a message. If your sellers do not hear from you for a while, they will call you. That will not be good. Do not wait for them to call. Even if you have nothing to say, **call anyway**!

Tell them nothing is happening. Ask if they have any thoughts or suggestions. Let them know you are still around, alive, working hard, and not off somewhere on vacation. You will find if you do **not** stay in touch, paranoia may set in, and they will make your life miserable.

## Important lessons in this chapter!

1. Each step in the sales process is a mini-sale. First sell the appointment; then move to the next step of selling for the listing. Look for opportunities to answer questions in such a way that it moves you to the next step.

2. Properly educate the seller so he knows what to expect and will work with you as a team.

3. Stay in touch!

# CHAPTER NINE
## Knock On Doors

To be a Super Salesman, you need to make things happen. One of the best ways to do that is to be face to face with a potential customer. What better way is there to find a customer than to knock on his door? The very best time to knock on doors is when you have a buyer that wants to live in a certain area. What an opportunity! Never let it pass! It is not often that you have an excuse to knock on someone's door!

Knock on the door, and simply introduce yourself, and tell the potential prospect that you have a buyer who would like to live in their area. Then ask if they would like to sell their property. If they say, "No," ask, "Who do you know in this area that is thinking of selling?" Notice that is not a "yes" or "no" question. Therefore, you can't be brushed off with a simple "no" answer.

For the most part, people like to be helpful. Once in a while, a house will have a sign that says, "No soliciting." In most cases, respect their wishes. Save that house until you have a customer who is looking for a house that looks similar to theirs, and there is a strong possibility they would buy it if it were for sale.

When you knock on that door, apologize for knocking then say you have a customer looking for a house in their neighborhood, and they like the looks of their home. Next ask if they are interested in selling.

Let me tell you an interesting story about knocking on doors. Once I had a wealthy man who had recently gotten a divorce and wanted to move into an upscale neighborhood. Up and down the street I went knocking.

Before long I knocked on a door, and the homeowner

said they were thinking of selling. They said they would discuss it overnight and let me know the next morning. The next day I listed the house. I showed it to my customer, but it didn't suit him. Fortunately for me, the house sold within a week.

When I knocked on the door right across the street, the lady invited me to come into her home. She told me they had purchased a lot out on a lake where they would eventually build their dream home.

She said ever since they bought the lot over three years ago, she wanted to sell the home they are living in and start building, but her husband wouldn't.

I asked if she would mind if I talked to her husband. She said, "Gladly, I wish you would." Before I left, she gave me her husband's work phone number. When I got back to the office, I called him and made an appointment to meet him at his office at 6 p.m., that evening.

Later in the afternoon, one of the sales ladies in my office asked me to help her put up a large commercial sign. After putting up the sign, we started back to the office.

I was still excited about my appointment scheduled for that evening, so I told her about finding the prospect by knocking on doors. Chapter 19 is titled: *Wisdom Nuggets*. In it is a subchapter titled: *The "Blabber Mouth."* After reading what happened next, you will understand why I gave it that title.

When I told her the name of the person I was dealing with, she said they were very good friends. As a matter of fact, they were in a bridge club together and played bridge every week. She said she had been working on listing their house for the last three years, ever since they had bought a lot on the lake.

Oh boy, that really put me in a dilemma. However, as

I thought about it, I decided that she wasn't really working on getting that listing. If she were, why did she never talk to the husband? She had three years of opportunity. Therefore, I concluded she was socializing, commenting every now and then; "Don't forget me when you get ready to sell." So, I went to the appointment and listed the house.

The next day, when she found out I had listed the house, she was furious with me and went to the broker and made a complaint. We all three sat down to discuss the situation. She presented her side. When it came to my turn, I said, "It comes down to this. I was working real estate, out knocking on doors. She, on the other hand, was playing real estate. For over three years, she had an opportunity to list the house."

The broker came down on my side. It caused a very cool relationship for about a month. Then this agent came to me and apologized. She said I was right. She agreed she had ample opportunity to list the house. She agreed she had not properly pursued the listing.

It took her a long time to get over being hurt because her friend listed with me instead of her. I thought she had a lot of character to say it was her own fault that she didn't get the listing. I am happy to say we are still very good friends.

When you read the Wisdom Nugget, about being a blabber mouth, remember this is just another reason not to discuss with others on what you are working. I have seen many sales agents in similar situations.

Had I gone to my appointment without blabbing it beforehand, it wouldn't have been an issue. Sure, she would have been disappointed that she didn't get the listing. However, she wouldn't have been upset with me because I wouldn't have known she had been, "so called," working on that listing.

Here is another story about knocking on doors. One day, I had nothing to do, so I decided to knock on some doors and try to list a few houses. At the first house, the man came to the door and told me he was a renter.

I said, "No-sir, you are really a buyer, buying this house for your landlord. He calls you a renter." He invited me in so we could talk further. In our conversation, I asked if he were looking to buy a house, what type house would it be. He pointed to the house directly across the street and said he had always liked the looks of that house.

I could hardly wait to get out of their house. I bet you know why. I left my car in the driveway and walked across the street and asked if they would like to sell their home. I told them I had a prospect for it. They said as a matter fact, they had talked about selling from time to time. I then had them sign a one-time showing/listing form and walked back across the street and told them we could go look at the house.

We looked at it and they liked it. I went back, and told the seller what the prospect thought about their home. I then signed them up on a long term listing agreement.

The customer I showed it to didn't buy. However, later I did sell it and sold that owner another house. Over the next several years, that owner listed, sold, and bought several houses. Now do you see how you can make things happen by knocking on doors?

**Important lessons in this chapter!**

1. When you think you have nothing else to do, you can always knock on doors.
2. Never pass up an opportunity to knock on doors, especially when you have a customer who wants a particular style house or neighborhood.

# CHAPTER TEN
## Asking and Answering Questions

Selling involves lots of questions. Sometimes **you** ask them, other times it is the buyer or seller that is asking. You may wonder why asking questions is so important in selling.

One reason is to find out what your customer wants or does not want. If you know what the customer wants it will be much easier to make the sale.

If a buyer says the price is too high, but you know he can afford it, distract that line of thinking by reminding him of what **he wants**. The more he thinks of what he wants, the less important the price becomes.

It could be living on a golf course or on a lake in the country; it could even be something as simple as large trees in the yard. Just get him to focus on what he wants instead of the price. Encourage him to talk, and the more he talks the better. This is an extremely important secret in becoming a Super Salesman.

When asked a question, after you find out what the person asking the question is thinking, always answer immediately and truthfully.

Find out what he wants first because it is never good to sell a feature until you know if the buyer wants it. For example, if you know that a house has a fireplace and the buyer ask, "Does this house have a fireplace?" Don't assume he want one. Before answering, ask "Do you want a fireplace?" If he says "no," only after you have answered that it does, should you attempt to sell him on why it may be a good feature to have.

There are many kinds of questions, as well as specific ways to ask or answer them. But first, let's talk about asking questions in general. In selling when you ask someone a question, if you are sure they heard and understood, **never** say anything until they have answered. That is especially true if it is an "**IS IT**" or "**CLOSING**" question. In a moment I will explain about these two kinds of questions.

Learn to ask the right thing at the right time and in the right way, and then wait for the answer. It is always good to answer a question by asking a question, especially a closing question. All this will be explained later in this chapter. These are skills you must practice to learn.

You should seldom ask a question that can be answered "yes" or "no." Notice; I didn't say never; I said seldom. It will take some thought and effort on your part to think and learn ways to ask questions. For instance, if you ask someone, "Do you know anyone who would be interested in buying a house," you will probably get a response of, "no."

Here is an example of how you could ask that same question without receiving a "no" answer. "Who do you know that may be interested in buying a house?" Notice, the person has to think before he can give you an answer. It cannot be answered "yes" or "no." Instead of asking, "Did you like the house?" Ask, "What did you like about the house, or what did you not like about it?"

In your social interactions with friends and family, start now to retrain yourself to rephrase your questions so they cannot be answered, "yes" or "no." Listen as people around you ask questions of one another. Listen to their responses. Often you will hear answers of "yes" or "no."

Think of how you could rephrase their question so it could not be answered that way. Do this until it instinctively becomes a part of how you think. Pause right here. Before reading any further, stop and think of questions you can ask that cannot be answered "yes" or "no."

Throughout this book, I will constantly talk about the questions you need to ask. You need to know how to ask them and why you should ask them in a certain way. Your question should never embarrass your customer or client. For example, **never** ask a customer how much they can afford. Rather, ask how much they would feel comfortable spending to buy a house or to spend for a house payment.

Many buyers do not want you to know they can only afford a small amount. They may tell you a higher figure to keep from being embarrassed. On the other hand, if you ask how much they want to spend, that will not be embarrassing to them. It leaves the assumption that they could spend more if they wanted to or if necessary.

Perhaps the most important questions you will ever ask are the "IS IT" questions and the "CLOSING" questions. You need to have a specific goal in mind when you ask either of them. First let me tell you what an "IS IT" question is.

It is a question where you ask: "Is it this, or is it that." That sounds simple enough doesn't it? It is an extremely important part of selling. It can be so powerful and important that I will devote a considerable amount of time on it in another chapter.

What is a CLOSING question? It is any question that moves you closer to and includes the final closing question. If you are trying to make an appointment, that is what you are selling. Usually there are many closing questions before you reach that goal. When you get the appointment, you have just made a sale.

The next sale comes while you are at the appointment. It may be to list or sell a house. Notice there is more than one sale before getting to the final sale. Each step you achieve is a sale. The first sale is just to get the person to talk to you. Next is a sale to make the appointment. Finally you sell the house or get the listing. That is the final sale.

Now, let's talk more about closing questions. When you ask a closing question and you are sure the customer understood the question, *__"SHUT UP,__*" and wait for their response. He or she who talks first loses. Thirty seconds may seem like an eternity, even if it is a minute or more just wait, smile, look them in the eyes, and wait.

Do not get nervous and start talking. This is the most critical part of the sale. It is real "subtle high-pressure" selling at its finest. It is not the kind of high-pressure where a salesman is trying to pressure someone into buying something they may or may not want. The kind of pressure I am talking about is when the salesman causes the customer to put pressure on himself to make a decision he is reluctant to make.

After I had almost finished writing this book, I was talking with a lady who was an author, teacher, editor, and publisher. I was asking questions about how to publish my book. When she found out my book was about selling, she said her father was a traveling salesman. Once a year, when she was a little girl, he would take her with him on the road for a week. It was some of her fondest memories. It was a time of excitement for her because they would eat in restaurants and stay in motels.

She said an unusual thing happened when he was selling. All of a sudden, everyone would stop talking; it was quiet for so long she felt uncomfortable. Then his customer would go over and get her purse and write a check. When she said that, I had to smile. I know what had happened. Her father must have been a good salesman and had asked a closing question. He knew when to stop talking.

60

Once I was negotiating on buying a dining room suite. I was talking to the owner of the furniture store, so I knew he could make the decision. I let him know I was willing to walk away from the sale. After a while, we reached a point where I thought I knew what the lowest price could be. It was a lot less than the Owner wanted. I said to him, "Will you take $1,800?"

It was a long time ago, and it was a very expensive piece of furniture. I looked him in the eyes, smiled, and waited for his answer. He squirmed, shifted from one foot to another and started making notes on a little notepad. Every once in a while he would look at me. I said nothing and continued to smile and look him in the eyes. After what seemed like an eternity, he meekly said, "Yes."

Even though I was the buyer, I was selling the seller. Remember earlier I said you do not always have to have a product to sell. It can be an idea or concept. In life we are always selling. Often we do not even realize it. In this sale, I was selling the seller on accepting a price lower than he wanted to accept.

It seems strange doesn't it, even though I was the buyer, I made the sale instead of the seller. I asked the closing question at the right time, in the right way, and kept my mouth shut until I got an answer. Learn how to do this and you will be very successful in closing sales and life in general.

Here is another example of how to use a closing question: The buyer may ask if the washer and dryer, stays with the house. You could answer with a strong closing question such as, "Would you be interested in this house if it does?"

Did you notice, without saying it, you just asked the buyer if he would buy the house if the washer and dryer, stays with it. By asking if he would be interested, it makes it easier for the buyer to say "yes." If he says "yes" he is telling you he will possibly buy this house.

Notice how easy it is for the buyer to say "yes" because of the way you answered his question with your own closing question. Always be thinking about how you can answer almost anything the buyer may ask with a closing question. This will probably not be natural for you. Therefore, you must put some thought and practice into it. In other words, you must always be thinking. I will now give an example of how I used a closing question to sell a house.

I had an offer in which the seller and buyer were in agreement on the price and terms. The only problem was the buyer wanted all the drapes to remain with the house. However, the seller wanted to keep them and move them to his new home.

The drapes were expensive, and the seller had overspent building his new home. He knew it would be very expensive to buy new drapes, so he wanted to keep the drapes and move them to his new house. On the other hand, the buyer didn't want to have the bother and expense of installing new drapes. I realized this could be a deal breaker, so this is how I handled it.

I went over the offer explaining it to the seller and laid the forms on the table with the pen. I told the seller he had the price and terms he wanted for his house. Notice I said house, this is no longer his home. I am trying to lessen the emotional attachment he has for this property. His home is now the new house he just built.

I reminded the seller that when he takes the drapes down they would need to be cleaned. I further stated after cleaning them, which is very expensive, who knows what condition they would be in after the cleaning process. In addition, I asked him if he knew whether they would fit the windows in his new home. Then I asked a strong closing question. My question was, "Are you going to let those old... used... drapes keep you from selling your house?"

Then I slid the offer across the table to him with the pen for his signature. I looked him in the eyes, smiled, and waited. I said nothing else because that was a strong closing question. I continued to look at him, smile, and wait.

After what seemed like an eternity, he picked up the pen and signed. His wife was thrilled beyond belief. All along, she had wanted new drapes. If I had said anything after asking that closing question, it would have taken the pressure away from him, and I probably would have lost the sale.

Notice, I didn't tell the seller what to do. I put it in proper perspective so he could think about it and make the decision. He had everything he wanted in the sale, except the drapes. That question, "Are you going to let those old, used, drapes prevent you from selling your house" put the ball in his court. It put pressure on him to make a decision that he was reluctant to make.

That is very subtle high-pressure selling! It is the kind of selling that helps people do what hopefully is in their own best interest.

There is another kind of high-pressure selling that gives salesmen a bad reputation. That is when the salesman tells the customer what to do and tries to pressure him into doing it. Both these techniques are high-pressure, but they are not both good.

In one, the salesman tells the customer what to do and tries to force him into doing it; that is bad. In the other, the salesman transfers the pressure to the customer. It is then that the customer puts pressure on himself to make his own decision; that is good. It is like a cowboy who drives his cattle versus the shepherd who leads his sheep.

This is high-pressure selling at its finest. Make sure you study, understand, and learn the difference in these two techniques. My way is a win-win situation for everyone. In this instance, the sale was made because I asked that closing question the right way and at the right time. I hope you noticed one of the most important things was that I kept my mouth shut until he responded. Doesn't that sound like fun?

## Important lessons in this chapter!

1. Learn to put pressure on without being a high-pressure salesman.

2. Always **think** when you are asking and answering questions.

3. When you ask a question do not keep talking just because you get nervous during a long pause. Wait for the answer, no matter how long it takes.

# CHAPTER ELEVEN
## "IS IT" Questions

As sure as night follows day, as you get near the closing you will encounter objections. It will be your job to determine if those objections are serious or just a stalling tactic because they are fearful. Keep in mind that many times buyers and sellers are scared, buyers probably more than sellers. Your job is to try to anticipate in advance any objection.

When you work with buyers, especially the first time buyer, they are afraid. This will perhaps be the largest financial transaction they will make in their lifetime. They are under great stress and will think of all kind of reasons not to buy.

Often when it's time to make the offer, they will usually say they want to think about it. For most salesmen that is the "kiss of death." Not for me, that is when I get out the nerve pills and start asking "**Is It**" questions. Remember the bottle of M&Ms from Chapter Three?

At this point in the sale, you will try to lessen their stress. So, agree with them. Tell them they should think about it and maybe even pray about it. After all, it is a very important financial decision for them to make. After you say that, pick up your briefcase and stand. They think you are about to leave. You can feel and almost see the tension as it leaves the room.

However, you are not about to leave. You are just getting ready to "set the hook." That doesn't mean you are about to do something unethical as will be explained in Chapter 13 on Ethics. It means you are about to close the deal, provided you have determined their objections are not serious and they are only stalling. Keep in mind, you already know they want to go through with the transaction; they are just scared. Now you need to find out if there are any real serious reasons not to proceed.

While you are standing, tell them you understand why they would want to think about it. After all, it is a very important financial decision for them. Then continue by saying, "To clear my thinking, what is it you want to think about?" Pause as if you are in deep thought but not long enough for them to start talking.

The next thing you do and say is **critical**. This is when you put down your briefcase, sit down, and immediately start asking "IS IT" questions. Once you say "IS IT," do not hesitate, start asking questions.

"Is It" the price? "Is It" the neighborhood? "Is It" the school district? "Is It" something about the house? "Is It" something else you haven't told me? "Is It" this, "Is It" that. You could develop a long list of "IS IT" questions and always be ready to use them.

At this point, the tension is gone and the buyer will probably start talking, telling you about their concerns. As soon as you find out what their concern or objection is do not ask anymore "Is It" questions. If you can find out what their objection is, you are in a better position to overcome it. Many times if their concerns are insignificant, you can continue with the closing.

Sometimes, they will say they want to discuss it with their parents, sibling, or friend. Keep in mind it may become very difficult to make the sale if they bring someone else into the sale. Therefore, you want to avoid that if possible.

You must proceed very cautiously but proceed you must. Never say anything negative about the person they want to ask for advice. Ask the buyer about the background of the person or persons they are looking to for advice. Find out if they have any expertise in real estate. Are they investors? Do they have building experience? If they have no experience in these areas and most do not, ask the buyer this question.

"Who would you go to for advice if you were going to buy a diamond?" Follow up by saying. "Hopefully, it would not be your friend the brick mason or your parent who may be an Accountant, Lawyer, Office Manager, Doctor, etc. Obviously, you would go to a jeweler." Then you might say; "Your parents love you and don't want you to make a mistake; that is why they almost always advise caution."

Then I say, "Unfortunately, often that is bad advice and could cause you to miss a good opportunity. Even though it may be on a subconscious level, your parents wouldn't want to be blamed if you did make a mistake. That is why the tendency is to urge caution. On the other hand, you have all the facts and they do not. They will be very proud that you are mature enough to make an adult decision on your own without involving them."

There are times that the objection of the buyer is important to them. Only if you know what the objection is can you help them make the right decision. It may be that the couple wants to discuss it between themselves. If so, agree that they should. Then excuse yourself to another room or step outside the house. Give them some time and privacy so they can find out if they are in agreement. But if possible, try to get the listing, or have them make the offer before you leave.

Tell the buyer they know as much about the offer right now as they will ever know. Reassure them they are making the right decision. Tell them you understand the real problem may be that they are afraid to make the offer which is normal. That is when you give the couple the container of M&M nerve pills. Ask them, "Which problem applies? Do you need to take one, two, or three of the chew only nerve pills?" After that they will usually laugh and sign the offer.

If they do not sign, tell them that in the morning, they will not know any more about the offer than they know right now, perhaps even less. The decision will still have to be made. So why spend a restless night tossing and turning worrying about it? Why not sign right now, and then get a good night's sleep?

I know this is almost more high-pressure than you would ever want to exert. However, sometimes a buyer may need reassurance, given a little shove, and be told what to do. That is especially true with first-time buyers. Be careful not to sound like the high-pressure salesman that is trying to get what he wants rather than what is best for them.

You never know what you may find out when you use "Is It" questions. Once, I had a couple that wanted a house in a certain area close to the Catholic school. They told me they were buying the house as an investment. When I started asking the "Is It" questions the man finally said; "Hoot we have not been totally honest with you. We are getting a divorce, and I am buying this house for my wife and children."

He wanted to make sure it was what she wanted before proceeding. I excused myself and gave them time to talk. When I came back into the room they were ready to proceed. Incidentally, more than once, I discovered that a couple was getting a divorce but were too embarrassed to tell me. Later, in my selling career, often I would know by instinct what the problem or objection was even before it surfaced.

Before leaving this chapter there are two final thoughts I want to impress on your mind. First, remember to ask what it is they want to think about, is it... Pause as if you are in deep thought, and start asking "Is It" questions. Ask them one after another until you find out what the objection is. Think of the various situations where "Is It" questions will need to be asked. Then build a very large repertoire of questions to ask so that you will be ready when the situation arises.

Next, anytime a buyer or seller says they want to pray about it respect that wish. Stop selling and make another appointment. If the property is good for them, they will probably get the answer they are looking for in their prayers. After that it will be a very easy sale. If they do not get the OK, it doesn't matter if you are the world's greatest Super Salesman; that is one sale you will not make!

## Important lessons in this chapter!

1.  Use "Is It" questions to find out what your customer is thinking. Read again in the paragraph above about how to use **critical** timing in asking the "Is It" questions.

2.  Anticipate objections, and have a list of "Is It" questions ready at all times.

3.  Sometimes you need to reassure and guide or even tell your customer what to do in making their decision. In those situations, don't be afraid to tell them what to do.

# CHAPTER TWELVE
## Do It Now

This story I love to tell. There are several lessons to be learned, and it will emphasize the importance of "doing it now." One hot July day in South Georgia, I took one of my agents out to give him some training. It must have been the hottest day of the year. We rode around in neighborhoods until we saw an owner's "For Sale" sign in his yard.

It was Saturday and the couple was home. My agent and I walked up to the house and introduced ourselves. The homeowners, realizing we were real estate sales agents, were not very receptive. I told them they were our biggest competition. Therefore, whether they sell their home or we sell it, I would like to see it sell right away. I said to them, "I have some ideas that will help you sell your home." I asked if we could come in out of the heat and discuss it.

That got their attention. They liked it that I was going to give them information on how to sell it. Therefore, we were invited into their home. We sat at the dining room table and talked. I didn't totally educate them on everything they needed to know about selling it, but I did give them a couple of good ideas.

Then I began selling them on why they should consider listing with us. I pointed out that most buyers will already have made contact with at least one real estate salesperson before they even get into town. Therefore, it would be a different kind of buyer that would be contacting them.

I told them they wouldn't know anything about the buyer who knocks on their door. They wouldn't know their motives or even if they are really motivated or financially qualified. I told them one thing they should know is that a buyer trying to deal directly with a seller is usually trying to save money. He knows you will not be paying a sales commission and that you have no one to protect your interest. You may also be trying to save the amount of the selling commission. Obviously you both can't save the commission. That means you are starting out from an adversarial position.

The reason the buyer is contacting you directly is because he is knowledgeable and confident. He wants to save the amount of the commission and even more. The question is who will get the savings? Will it be you, the seller or the buyer?

I asked them how much experience they had in selling houses. Since they had no experience, I said it will probably be the buyer. He will know what he is doing and try to drive a hard bargain.

I explained why they needed a professional in their corner. I know of far too many sales where an owner thought they had sold their home and moved. Then the buyer moved in on a rental basis until closing. The next thing you know, the deal falls apart before it closes. You cannot imagine the heartache and expense that would be. In addition, it could cause them to sell again at a much lower price causing a huge loss.

I told them if they listed the house with us, they could possibly make as much or more than if they sold it themselves. That could be true even after paying a commission. Because we are more skilled at negotiating, buyers will usually pay more when buying through a professional real estate agent. They seemed very receptive and after asking all the closing questions, I was sure we would get the listing.

They said they wanted to think about it. Therefore, I asked a lot of "IS IT" questions. Still they wanted to think about it. I knew they needed to discuss it privately to be sure they were in agreement. So, I told them we would step into the garage and give them some time to talk to one another.

When we got outside, I told my agent I was very confident they would call us back in within a few minutes, and they would list their home with us. I also told him, to be on the safe side, I left my briefcase inside by my chair. That way, I would have an excuse to go back into the house. It would give me one more opportunity to close the deal if they did not list.

It was now about 1:30 p.m. in the afternoon. It was hot, and we were wearing suits and ties. We immediately began to sweat like pigs. We waited 10 minutes, 20 minutes, 30 minutes, and longer. Finally the man came to the door and said they had decided to wait awhile.

I was very surprised because I thought I did an outstanding presentation, and they seemed receptive. It was almost funny to see the look on my agent's face. After that long sweaty wait, we were not going to get the listing.

I thanked the man and said I needed to step back inside to get my briefcase. I was thinking, "It took them too long." They were having a conflict, and I needed to find out what it was. I knew they wanted to list, but something was holding them back.

When I went back into the house, the wife had already left the room. I asked the husband if he would get her. When she came in, I asked what made them decide not to list. I don't even remember what their objection was; however, that is not the reason for this story. Whatever the objection, I overcame it and listed the house right then.

Just before leaving, I took down the sign they had in their yard and replaced it with mine. As I started to return to my car, I noticed a car with a real estate sign on the side of it drive by slowly. The real estate agent in the car was looking at my sign. They stopped and looked at the house. Within an hour the buyer with that sales agent placed a contract on the house.

We made a very handsome commission that day. It was because I had the foresight to leave my briefcase in the house. This allowed me to have a second attempt at listing it. Another reason is because we did it **now.** We didn't write down the address with the intention of coming back later.

There you see why it is so important to always "**do it now**." The term for that is "Time is of the essence." Had we decided to come back to that house later, the other sales agent would have seen the owner's "For Sale" sign, not mine. She would have made the sale directly with the owner, and we wouldn't have participated in it.

Here is another example of why you should always do it now. Several years before I retired from the Air Force, I was an Air Force Recruiter. There was a young Lieutenant that worked in our Detachment office in Jacksonville, Florida. He helped support the recruiters, I would see him often, and we would talk. We did not socialize outside of work, but we were friendly and often chatted with one another.

A couple of years later, I was transferred to recruit in North Carolina; he was transferred to the University of North Carolina as the ROTC Instructor. We ran into each other and re-established our friendship. Later, I was transferred to Warner Robins, Georgia. Can you believe I ran into him again at a restaurant after a New Year's Eve party?

Years later, he moved to Valdosta, Georgia, where I was working as a real estate salesman. In Valdosta, we again re-established our friendship. I formed several partnerships of investors to purchase and rent residential houses. He joined one of the Partnerships. I tell you all this to let you know even though we didn't socialize, he was more than just an acquaintance.

A few years later he decided to leave Valdosta and needed to sell his home. Naturally he contacted me. That should have been an easy house for me to list, and I probably was a little overconfident. He had a certain price in mind, but I had done my research and knew it was too high.

I tried to convince him to lower the price. He told me he would think about it and let me know. Two days later, I drove by his house, and there was a competitor's real estate sign in his yard. Honestly, I was shocked.

The house was listed at the price the owner wanted. A month or so later, it sold for a little less than the price I had suggested. Even though it sold near my price, I didn't get a payday. After the house closed out, I went to him. I reminded him we had been friends for several years. We were even in a Partnership together. I asked him to be "brutally honest" with me and not to spare my feelings.

I said, "Since I now make my living selling real estate, I need to learn what I did wrong." I am glad I asked. He said he told me the price he wanted and I was negative about it. The next day when he went to his office, he told his secretary about our meeting. What I didn't know is his secretary's daughter was a real estate agent who worked in a company across town. His secretary suggested he give her a call. The rest is history.

There were several lessons I learned.

- The first lesson I thought I already knew. **Do it now!**

- The second lesson was something I did for the rest of my real estate selling career. Here is how I handled those situations where the owner wanted more than the house was worth. I would tell them **only once** their price was too high. I didn't dwell on it. I would say selling real estate is not an exact science. Therefore we will try selling it at your price. We can always change it later if necessary.

  After getting the listing, I would go back to the sellers and tell them what other sales agents were saying when they viewed their house. I would also tell them what buyers were saying when they were shown the house. That way, I am not the bad guy. It is the other agents and buyers saying the listing price is too high. I would get the listing **now** and make price changes later if necessary.

- The third lesson is: *you don't know what you don't know*. Had I known my friend's secretary's daughter that was a competitor agent, I probably would have handled the situation differently.

## Important lessons in this chapter!

1. Very important, if you go outside to give your customer privacy, leave something in the house. It will give you one more opportunity to go back for another attempt to close the sale.

2. The most important lesson of all is get the listing now, and if necessary, make price adjustments later. "Never put off until tomorrow what can be done today!" Time is always of the essence in selling.

# CHAPTER THIRTEEN
## Ethics In Selling

In the fifth paragraph of Chapter 11, I made a comment about getting ready to "set the hook." If that caused you to raise your eyebrows, it should have. It sounded like I was going to tell you to take advantage of the buyer by using high-pressure to get what you wanted rather than what was in their best interest. That was not the case.

When you work with your customer, you should try to establish rapport and make a friend. If you do a good job of it, you will have a tremendous amount of influence in helping them to make decisions.

Sometimes, you will get to know the buyer so well you will know what they want, need, and is in their best interest. You will both know. Still, even though they know what they should do, it will be difficult for them because they are unsure or afraid. Thus, they are reluctant to make the decision. This part of selling is exciting, but it is also scary. That's because there will be times you may feel like you are playing God.

It is uncanny how much influence you sometimes have on customers. You do not want to influence them into doing something that will be a mistake and hurt them. This brings up the point of "Ethics in Selling." Physicians have an oath called the "Hippocratic Oath." It is a Latin phrase "Primum non nocere." It means "First, do no harm." All salesmen, especially real estate salesmen, should work under a similar oath.

Never forget the main reason for being honest and ethical is it's the right thing to do! Not only is it the right thing, it is good business. A study was done at a major university, and it was determined that 81% of buyers buy because they trust the integrity of the salesman.

Sometimes you will need to tell a customer what to do, and you need them to trust you enough to do it. Over time, in many ways, you will benefit because people trust you. There is another compelling reason for doing the right thing; it is in your best interest.

Your honesty and good ethics will determine how hard you will have to work throughout the rest of your selling career. If you are dishonest and do what is only in your best interest, you may make some sales. However, what may be good for you in the short run could be terrible for you in the long run. Your reputation of being dishonest and unethical will spread.

You will have to work hard for the rest of your life. Every sale you make will be a one-time sale. Your customers will not come back to you. Neither will they send their friends, relatives, or acquaintances to you. Without their repeat business, you will never become a Super Salesman.

No matter how tempting, never use your influence to the customer's detriment just to make a buck. I emphasize this because when the commission is several thousand dollars, you may be tempted. However, never yield to the temptation of cutting corners and doing whatever is necessary to make the sale. I have seen salesmen say or do almost anything to make a sale. I'm sure you have seen them too. In every case, they were mediocre salesmen, and will never be more than that.

Never think about the money you will earn on any sale. Make service your goal, and the money will follow. That's because if you do what is in your customer's best interest, they will come back and do business with you again. Not only that, they will send their friends, relatives, and acquaintances to you.

They will come back for you to sell their property, or they may buy again. It is not unusual for someone to live in a house for a few years and then get transferred out of town. They will need to sell. You want them to have confidence and trust in you so they will call you.

In addition, you can make another fee by referring the seller to an out of town salesmen where they are moving. Many times they may want to upgrade as their financial circumstances improve or as their family grows. They may need a larger house. Or they may need to downsize. That will mean two sales. Sell the old house, and then sell them a new one. You may do many transactions over the years with the same person.

Because of your honesty, many people will be referred to you over time. After you get these referrals, you need to educate them to refer their friends and relatives to you.

When they make referrals to you, you will start out having credibility with these new customers. They will trust you because you have gained a reputation of being trustworthy. Also, the one who recommended them to you will have told them you are trustworthy.

As the years go by your income will increase, and your job will become easier. That's because you will have built a network of buyers, sellers, and centers of influence. I will have more to say on this in the last chapter titled: *How to Become a Super Salesman.*

Always remember honesty is by far the best policy. That is a "no brainer!"

**An important lesson in this chapter!** Like I said, "It's a no brainer!" Build your business and reputation on honesty and integrity; it's good business!

# CHAPTER FOURTEEN
## "Outside the Box"

A part of being successful is being willing to accept opportunities and challenges as they arise. That means you will have to step out of your comfort zone. It helps you develop your creativity. Once you have accepted a challenge you must persevere to the end. Greatness comes in never quitting.

In this chapter, I will give you some ideas on how to be creative in putting deals together. You can use these ideas in selling or investing. The main thing is to develop an attitude that **"There is always a way!"** Like a mystery or puzzle, it's up to you to figure out the answer. Once you have an idea or challenging opportunity, you must think and figure out a way to make it happen.

Some of the deals to be discussed in this chapter didn't always involve large sums of money. Even so, they happened to be some of the more interesting and creative deals I have put together. It is up to you to learn how to think so you will be in a position to take advantage of opportunities as they arise.

My intention is to start you down the path of accepting challenges and being creative. It will be up to you to expand on these ideas. The more you tackle unfamiliar challenges, the more creative you will become. In addition, you could read books, watch videos, attend seminars, and brainstorm with other successful salespeople. Always look for ideas, and above all **think** about how you can creatively apply these ideas to your various sales or investment situations.

Growing up poor, my ambition was to move into the upper middle class financially. Therefore, I did some investing before I retired from the military. Without having a lot of financial resources, I was constantly looking for ways to maximize my investments. It's not easy to go to a bank and get loans for investment purposes.

I learned about second mortgages, land sale contracts, wrap around mortgages, and even bartering. If you are unfamiliar with these methods of investing, you can look them up on the INTERNET. You can use these methods to help you put deals together for your buyers and sellers as well as for your own personal investing.

I learned how to use leverage in buying, being careful not to overextend myself. Years later, all of this paid off when I started selling real estate. I was knowledgeable and astute at putting deals together. You can do the same.

Before continuing this chapter I want to give you a few definitions. A **note** is the promise to pay. A **mortgage** puts the property up as collateral to guarantee the payment of the note. In the remainder of this book, sometimes I may say note, or I may say mortgage. Other times I may say note with mortgage. In all these cases I will be talking about the same thing. Basically it means there is still money owed and will be paid, usually in payments over many years.

One of my very first sales involved a note with a second mortgage. It was fairly straight forward. I had a young couple with $3,000. It was not enough to pay the seller's asking equity of $5,000. I wrote up the offer with the buyer assuming the first mortgage already on the house and paying 3,000 cash. The buyer then offered to give the seller a note with a second mortgage for the remaining 2,000 at 6% interest.

The seller wouldn't take a note as part of the down payment. He wanted all his cash at closing. I asked if he would accept $4,500 if he got it all in cash. When he said yes, I told him to accept the offer because I would buy the note from him for $1,500. That gave him $3,000 from the buyer and $1,500 from me. Therefore, he got his $4,500 equity.

The buyer bought the house which earned me a commission of over $1,500. I used my commission to buy the $2,000 note. Where else could I have invested $1,500 and have an instant $500 profit? Since the 6% interest was paid on the $2,000 note instead of the $1,500 I had invested, my yield was not 6%; it was 8%.

By being creative, I was able to make the sale, enabling the buyer to purchase when he otherwise would have been unable to buy. Also, it helped the seller to sell and gave me a good investment. Now that was a win-win-win situation for everyone involved in the transaction.

Disclosure is extremely important in a transaction like this where you are personally involved. All parties involved, buyer, seller, and the broker must be told in writing what your involvement is in the transaction.

Let's take this a step further. You may think you cannot afford to invest your commissions that way. Maybe you can! At the time I made this sale in the late 1970s, I could borrow from the bank for much less than 8% interest. As I write this book, you can borrow for even a lower percentage. **You are money ahead** if you can borrow money from the bank for a lower rate than you receive in your creative deals. That's what is called using "Other People's Money" or OPM. Read those last two sentences again.

To get started, develop a relationship with a Banker. Then set up a "line of credit" (LOC) with the bank. The cost to set it up is negligible compared to the many fees you would pay for a home loan. Using the transaction just mentioned, I could have used the $2,000 note as collateral to get a better interest rate.

To make your deals more attractive to the Banker so he will give you a better interest rate, set it up so the mortgage payments on your investments will be paid directly to the bank. Do not be concerned that the payments are going to the bank instead of directly to you. The payment will be used to reduce the amount owed to the bank.

If you need money to live on, you can make a draw from your LOC. Remember, you will pay less interest to the bank than you are earning on your investment. Also the bank will be applying the mortgage payments to reduce the amount owed on your LOC loan. If you do not have a balance owed, the payments would go directly into your personal account.

As a salesman your income is not steady. There will be times you may be living by borrowing from your LOC. The interest rate on the LOC is almost always higher than the rate earned on your savings account. Therefore, always use any extra income to reduce the LOC before placing money into your savings.

In the beginning you may want to make your LOC for about $10,000. You can increase it to a higher amount later if needed. Initially, you may not get the very best rate, but over a short period of time, you may be able to get a much better rate. After many years, I got my rate down to between zero and 1/4% over the bank prime rate.

If you put the right kind of solid deals together, you could live off your LOC and continually invest your commissions into buying notes. You have little to worry about as long as you're earning a higher return than you are paying the bank. Unfortunately, not enough of your transactions will afford you the opportunity to make those kinds of investments. However, as you gain more experience and knowledge, you can let your fellow sales agents know that you would consider helping them to make sales by investing in some of their transactions.

**A note of caution!! It takes a special kind of disciplined person to live by borrowing from their Line of Credit (LOC). Never ever borrow from your line just because it is available. Also, never overextend yourself by borrowing to the point your payment to the bank would be more than your monthly investment income such as rent or mortgage payments you are receiving. Most importantly, if you are not disciplined in personal financial matters, do not attempt to live by borrowing from a LOC!!**

Now back to the deal I was just discussing; I could have continued to be creative. For instance, the $2,000 note I bought for $1,500 is something of value. It could be used every time an opportunity arose such as collateral for borrowing money. It could be bartered, traded, or even sold. For example, say I bought a property requiring a $7,000 down payment. There's a possibility the seller would take my note as part of the down payment. It could be used when buying almost anything of value, even a car.

Changing the subject for a moment, which do you think is more important, price or terms? I am going to make some big exaggerations to show it can be either. For instance, if you buy a property that is worth and could immediately be sold for $100,000 and you buy it for $40,000 you may think you got a fantastic deal. What if it only cost $15,000? That would be even better. This may make you think that price is more important than terms. However, there is a saying; *I will pay your price if you will accept my terms.*

Here is another exaggerated example: Would you pay two million dollars for an income producing property that is only worth $100,000? Think about it before you answer. My answer is, "Yes, I would buy it." Here are my terms. Ten dollars down, 4% interest for 99 years. The payment is $1.00 per year with a balloon payment. All principal and interest would be due at the end of the term of 99 years.

Bring them to me; I will buy all I can get. Learn these concepts because you can use them over and over in various creative ways. Use and modify them to suit the situation.

Let me tell you about another of my early creative investments. The year I became a real estate salesman, I met a rich elderly woman who wanted to liquidate all her real estate holdings. She offered to sell me one of her houses. It was a huge old house with a very wide dogtrot hallway in the middle running from front to rear.

She had converted it into two apartments, one on each side of the hallway. One side had two bedrooms, the other side had one. The hallway was used as a sitting room for both apartments. She said she would finance it for a very reasonable interest rate and I only had to pay her $1,000 down payment.

She further stated that each apartment was rented to a widow. Those elderly ladies had lived there for over twenty years. The rent was $30 for one side and the other was $20, which was unbelievably low rent. She said she had never gone up on the rent because "It is my benevolence."

I told my boss about the house and that I was thinking of buying it. He said I should not buy because it was located in a bad section of town. Remember what I said in a paragraph above about terms? My thinking was, I would only have $1,000 invested, and I could increase the rent substantially over time. The rent alone would pay back the thousand dollar investment and more, so I bought it.

When I met the tenants, the first thing they said was they knew I would have to increase the rent. They asked me not to increase it too much. So, I increased the $30 side to $45 and the $20 side to $30. My two tenants were thrilled because it was still grossly under the market rent. Over the next several years as their social security payments increased each year, I increased their rent a little. That way it did not cause them a hardship.

After several years, the rent was up to a decent amount even though it was still way under market rent. I then went to the bank and borrowed $12,000. The bank took back a second mortgage on the house as collateral. I used the money to buy three investment rental houses. They were only a few years old and in a much better area.

Just a few years earlier, those houses had been bought new by veterans. They used their VA entitlement which meant they bought them with no down payment. Also, the houses had long term assumable low-interest rate loans. Because the veterans didn't have to pay a down payment, they were willing to sell for less equity. That is why the $12,000 was enough to buy all three.

Later, I got to thinking the old house would need extensive repairs in the near future so I decided to sell it. I wanted to do some creative financing in order to maximize my profit when it sold. However, the second mortgage I had placed on it when I borrowed the $12,000 would prevent me from being very creative.

Therefore, I went to my banker and asked if he would transfer their second mortgage from the old house to one of the newer ones I had bought with the $12,000. His first response was they had never done that. I explained that the house I wanted to transfer the mortgage to was newer and in a better area. He said, "No."

He said he would gladly give me a new loan to pay off the second mortgage on the old house and place that mortgage on one of the newer houses. I told him I would not do that because interest rates had increased. I asked if he was sure he wanted to keep the old house as collateral.

I told him I was willing to move the collateral to a newer, more valuable house in a much better area. I gave him the addresses of both the old and the newer house. I asked him to go look at them before making the final decision. Later that afternoon, he called and said he would transfer their bank loan to the newer house. See how being creative pays off!

Then, I sold the old house for a substantial profit. I got $2,500 cash down and a note with a wrap around mortgage as security for the balance. Even though much of my profit was tied up in the wrap around mortgage, it was earning a high interest rate, thus giving me a profitable payment. The payment on it was enough to pay the payment on the wrap mortgage with money left over.

I now had two and a half times my original thousand dollars back. Also I had three other investment rental houses plus the wrap around mortgage. In addition, I made several thousand dollars profit from the rental income of the old house over the several years I owned it. There was also the tax advantage of depreciation.

Over time, the wrap mortgage **payments were** enough to pay off the underlying first mortgage. At that point, the wrap mortgage became the 1st mortgage, meaning all future payments were mine to keep. Later I used that note and mortgage as a down payment in purchasing yet another house.

Many years later the mortgages on those investment houses had been paid down substantially. They were paid down by my renters. Over the years, I had gotten tremendous tax advantages by owning them. When I sold them, each house had appreciated in value by tens of thousands of dollars. In addition, the amount owed was reduced by thousands of dollars. Not bad for my original $1,000 investment.

Another creative sale I made was a complicated sale involving three houses and three Owners. That was perhaps one of the more creative and difficult transactions I ever made. It may be difficult for you to understand and see the complications this sale presented to me. Unfortunately, by reading about it instead of being there, you will not get the same experience, the fun, the excitement, and the thinking processes that allowed me to move this sale from one step to the next.

I am going to lay it all out from the beginning. This was one of those deals you would have enjoyed more if you could have been there to see how it unfolded. To appreciate it the way I did, you would have had to experience it. After all this time, it still excites me to think about it. Enough of my reminiscing now read and learn. There are several important lessons to be learned.

To understand this transaction, you may need to read it slowly, one sentence at a time, and think as you read. Do not go on to the next sentence until you clearly understand the sentence you just read.

Early in my selling career, I had an owner who wanted to sell his house and buy a more expensive house a short distance away. He had already been talking to the owner of the house he wanted to buy. Let's start by calling the first owner, Owner A. The owner of the house that Owner A wanted to buy, I will call, Owner B.

I listed Owner A's house and went to talk to Owner B. The two owners had been talking to one another for almost a month. It turned out Owner B wanted to buy a much larger and more expensive house a few blocks away.

He had been talking with that owner. I will call him Owner C. The problem was Owner B could not buy Owner C's house until his house sold. Owner A could not buy Owner B's house until his house sold. Next I went to talk to Owner C. He told me he was downsizing and had bought a condo and was getting ready to move into it in a couple of weeks. Are you confused yet? Just wait, it will get much more complicated. Buckle your seat belt, and hang on as we travel on down this road.

In order to put this deal together, I told Owner C he could buy Owner A's house and immediately place it back on the market to sell. Owner A could then buy Owner B's house, and Owner B could buy Owner C's. Owner C would get enough money from the sale of his house to pay cash for Owner A's. He would even have money left over.

I pointed out if he didn't do this in a couple of weeks he would have a large, empty, and expensive house to sell. It would make more sense to have a smaller less expensive house on the market. It would probably take less time to sell, and it would be less costly to maintain while it was being sold.

This may not be necessary; however, if you feel it would be helpful to assist in following one step to the next, a drawing may help. Get out a piece of paper, and draw a simple outline of three houses. Label the houses as follows: The first house is Owner A's, the second, Owner B's, and the third, Owner C's.

Use the drawing of the three houses if needed to follow this transaction. You can make notes and draw arrows between the houses as I give you the facts. Try not to get lost as we travel down this road together. Check your seat belt because ahead are several curves. Now the fun begins!

To make it work, I told Owner C I wouldn't charge a commission when he bought Owner A's house. It would be deferred until it resold. If no commission was paid on Owner A's house, it would give a windfall to him. Because of that, we reduced the price Owner C paid for Owner A's house by the amount of the commission. It would then be placed back on the market at the original price which would include a commission when I sold it again. Now I am going to further complicate the deal.

Slow down, take as much time as you need to understand and follow each step in these transactions. Think as you move through each step. Owner A did not have a loan on his house. The loan on Owner B's house was at 9% interest and it had a "due on sale" clause.

That means the bank could either increase the interest rate when the house sold or call the loan due. The loan on Owner C's house was a much larger loan and had an interest rate of 6½%. Fortunately, it didn't have a "due on sale" clause. That means Owner C could sell his house and allow the buyer to assume his 6½% loan without the bank's approval.

These three sales took place in the early 1980s when interest rates went out the roof. The interest rate for most home loans with discount points figured in was calculated to provide a yield to the lender of approximately 23%. Even the largest corporations had to pay the prime rate; which at that time was hovering near 20% or more.

Surprisingly and fortunately both Owner B's and Owner C's loans were held by the same bank. That made it easier with only one bank in which to negotiate. The Banker was a very negative and straight by the book type person. He didn't have a creative bone in his body. Even so, he was a good banker, just overly protective of his bank. I knew I had my work cut out for me. Because he was so negative and pessimistic, I am going to call him "Ole Doom & Gloom."

In order for Owner A to buy Owner B's house, Owner A needed to assume Owner B's loan which had the "due on sale" clause. "Ole Doom & Gloom" was not willing to let Owner A assume it unless the interest rate was increased to 19%. That was a deal breaker, and "Ole Doom & Gloom" wouldn't budge on the 19% rate.

I puzzled over how I could make this deal work. It represented three sales for me, and there were no listing agents involved. That meant I would get both the listing and selling commissions. It would be big to sell three houses at the same time, especially since I would be getting both sides of the commission.

For several days I deliberated over what I could do to put this sale together. Even in church the next Sunday morning, no matter how hard I tried, I could not get this transaction out of my mind. My Pastor says "Confession is good for the soul but bad for the reputation."

So, I must confess. It was in church when I had my "Eureka" moment. I was thinking; I have three buyers and sellers that want to buy and sell. Terms and prices were all in agreement. There just had to be a way!

The only problem was "Ole Doom & Gloom." I forgot about the buyers and sellers and started thinking about what I could do to make "Ole Doom & Gloom" allow Owner A to assume Owner B's loan without increasing the interest rate to 19%. That was the main problem holding up the deal. Suddenly it hit me. Finally! I had the answer. I jumped straight out of my pew and shouted! NO NOT REALLY, but if I had, I bet that really would have stirred up the service!

The next day I went to Owner B and asked if he would

be willing to assume the 6½% mortgage on Owner C's house and allow the bank to increase it to a rate of 9%, even though it did not have a "due-on sale" clause. I pointed out that it was still a much lower rate than if he were to get a new loan. I told him I thought I could make the deal go through if he would agree. Without hesitation, he agreed; hallelujah!

Remember earlier in this chapter I told you about substituting the collateral for a loan on one house by transferring it to another? I am going to use that same kind of thinking to do something similar. Only this time, it will involve the manipulating of interest rates between loans. Now, I was off to see "Ole Doom & Gloom."

I asked him to let Owner A assume the 9% loan without invoking the bank's "due on sale" clause. As compensation for allowing the assumption without changing the rate, Owner B would assume the 6½% loan and allow the bank to raise the rate to 9%, even though it did not have a "due on sale" clause. I pointed out to him that the loan at 6½% was much larger than the 9% loan with the due on sale clause. Therefore, that was a good deal for the bank.

Then I told him the alternative was to accept the fact that he was going to have that larger 6½% loan for the next 20 years because it did not have a "due on sale" clause. I emphasized that no one was going to pay it off early when they could assume it at such a low rate.

When I presented it to him that way, I noticed he was beginning to warm up to the idea. I think it is the first time I ever saw "Ole Doom & Gloom" get excited about anything. Before I left, we were both about to shout.

All three sales closed at the same time using the same attorney. That was because if any one of the sales fell through, they would all fall.

You may not appreciate the complexity of this sale the way I did because you have a script to follow. However, I had no script. I was flying by the seat of my pants. I had to think and do each step one at a time as I thought of various ways to make it happen. That is how you do creative things. You accept the challenge, and then figure out a way to make it happen.

Now let's talk about the lessons learned. First and foremost where there is a will, there almost always is a way. It is up to you, the salesman, to make it happen. Remember, you are the catalyst. You must **think** long and hard and **never quit**. The second lesson is to tackle any challenge, and do not be afraid to go outside your comfort zone. In other words, think "outside the box." The third lesson is one I have not yet told you.

It is this: as part of the closing of the three houses, I listed the house that Owner C bought. I insisted that the attorney place a special stipulation in the listing agreement that said "coupled with an interest." That is a very important stipulation.

It means I had a financial interest in the house Owner C bought. Therefore, he could not arbitrarily revoke my listing. My interest being the earlier commission I had deferred. Even in the event of the owner's death, the listing would not be revoked.

"Coupled with an interest" is a term few real estate agents know about or use. Sometimes attorneys use it with a "power of attorney" to extend the term of the power. If it is ever challenged in court, the document will not stand up unless there actually is an interest.

Therefore, use it only when you do have an interest in a transaction in which you have been involved. Not always but usually it is when you have deferred a commission until some future event happens. Remember the term "**coupled with an interest**." Use it when appropriate.

Interestingly, a short time after those three houses closed, I got a call from a young couple that wanted to see the house I had put back on the market to sell for Owner C. I showed it to them, and they fell in love with it and wanted to buy it. The only problem was; you guessed it. They had to sell their home first. I thought, "Oh boy! Here we go again." Since Owner C was already educated I thought, "Why not give it a try." When I called Owner C, he said: "Oh no, not again!"

I pointed out to him that he would get another chunk of his money, and it would be less expensive to hold the even smaller house while waiting for it to sell. I also told him it was probably a more salable house. It was more in a range where investors would consider buying it as a rental. Thus, there would be more buyers for it. Owner C said he didn't want to go through that ordeal again. However, I talked him into looking at the house.

It was a small cute two bedroom house in a very good area, only about three blocks away. When Owner C looked at the small house he really liked it and thought he might make the trade and keep it as a rental investment. While he was considering it, unfortunately for the young couple, but fortunately for Owner C, another offer came in and his house sold. That ended the sale of the A, B, and C circle of houses! End of story.

## Important lessons in this chapter!

1. Often selling involves solving people's problems. Consider it an opportunity, and be willing to accept challenges and work diligently attempting to solve them. The reward for success is great!
2. **Thinking** is a big part of being creative.
3. Never give up; persevere to the end.

# CHAPTER FIFTEEN
## Staying Motivated

Being motivated and focused is an important part of selling. In an earlier chapter, I mentioned that you could read motivational books. In addition, there are CD's you can listen to in your car; what better time is there for you to listen to them? You are sitting there driving with nothing else to do, so why not make the time productive?

Please do not use that time to make your phone calls or text. That is too much distraction and is dangerous. Here is an example of how a motivational CD, book, or anything motivational can help you to succeed.

When I first became an Air Force recruiter it wasn't a very hard job. We just waited until someone was about to get drafted into the Army; then the person would come to us to join the Air Force. A short time later, the "draft" was eliminated. We had just converted to an all-volunteer force, and it was the recruiter's job to make it work.

This happened at the height of the Vietnam War. Then it became a difficult task. Rioting was taking place in the streets and on college campuses. Those young people were rioting trying to end the war. It was a time of "hippies" and "drugs." Military recruiters were hated. Some recruiting offices were even bombed.

Our largest market to recruit was the high school graduate. We would go to the schools and get a computer list of all the seniors with their phone numbers. Then we would call and try to sell them on joining the Air Force. It was a numbers game.

Sometimes we would have to call as many as 50 students to find one that had a slight interest. Then we would attempt to sell that one on joining. You can see it was hard work. Also, it was practically impossible to do without the list of seniors with their phone numbers.

It happened that one of the principals of a large high school in my recruiting area hated the war and the military. He hated the draft even more. He wouldn't allow anyone in his school to give out a list of the seniors. I was warned about him when I took over the area. Even so, I went to him and pleaded with him to give me a list. It was to no avail.

Now I will digress for a moment to tell you another story and then come back to this one. Often I listened to motivational tapes and recordings. One night I listened to a recording of Charlie Cullen's giving a motivational speech. He told about a national convention where he was hired to give the keynote address. There were several thousand salesmen in attendance.

The hotel where the convention was held had a large ballroom upstairs. They had put down an artificial ice skating rink and were putting on an ice show. He said one evening after all the events ended for the day, he decided to go up and see the ice show. When he opened the door to the ballroom, he saw that it was packed. He asked the usher if they had room for just one more. The usher said, "No, it wasn't possible."

Charlie said he was disappointed as he went back down to the lobby. When he entered the lobby, one of his friends came up to him and said, "Let's go up and see the ice show." Charlie started to tell him it was sold out and not possible.

Then a devilish thought occurred to him. He said this man was a top salesman and always got the sale. So Charlie thought he would like to see how he would react when he realized he could not make this sale. So he said, "Great, let's go see the show, lead the way!"

When they got to the ballroom and opened the doors, his friend saw they were filled beyond capacity. He turned to Charlie and said, "Follow me!" He strode down the aisle and looked like he was about to sit down somewhere when the usher came rushing up to him. He turned and looked at the usher and stuck up two fingers, and in a very stern, loud, and commanding voice said "**Two!**"

Charlie said that was not an inquiry; it was a command! Somewhere out of the back room the usher found a very small table, just big enough for two glasses and two chairs. As Charlie settled down into his chair, he thought, "What just happened? I was here five minutes earlier, and they didn't have room for even one. Then, when my friend comes in they find room for twice as many."

So, what was the difference? Charlie said he had gone up to inquire about how business was, but his friend had gone up **to see the ice show!**

Now back to my story about the high school principal. As I was driving my car back to Jacksonville, Florida, from St. Augustine, I began thinking about Charlie and the ice show story. I got so fired up thinking about it that I could not wait to get to that school to talk to the principal again. I decided I was not going to make an inquiry! Like Charlie's friend, I was going to get that list!

The first thing I did was to ask the principal what he thought of the Vietnam War. Of course, I knew what he would say. He told me in no uncertain words he was opposed to it. Then I asked what he thought of the draft. He was even more opposed to it.

I told him the military was not going away. I pointed out that recruiters had to have the list of seniors in order to make the all-volunteer force work. I said, "You cannot have it both ways. If we don't succeed in making the all

96

volunteer force work, the draft will come back." Since he liked the idea of the all volunteer force better than the draft, I got the list.

Later, some of my fellow recruiters could not believe I had gotten the list of seniors. They asked how I did it. I just smiled and said, "I'm a Salesman." In my mind I thought, "Thanks Charlie!"

## Important lessons in this chapter!

1. Motivation and enthusiasm will cause you to do things you thought were impossible.
2. Remember where there is a will; there almost always is a way. You just have to find it.

# CHAPTER SIXTEEN
## The Orchestrated Close

I did not learn about the "Orchestrated Close," until late in my selling career. I wish I had known about it earlier. I don't remember where I heard about it.

Perhaps I read about it, saw it in a video, or heard about it in a seminar. It was interesting so I decided to give it a try. I found it to be powerful, extremely effective, and fun.

It can be effective in almost any selling situation. However, it is most effective when you have a buyer and seller of the same temperament negotiating on a property. I am talking about a seller that is almost fanatical about getting every last dollar possible for the sale of his property, which includes many sellers.

The buyer on the other hand doesn't want to pay even one dollar more than necessary, again many buyers. Therefore, almost every offer will be countered. Then the counteroffer will be countered. Back and forth it goes. This is an example where you truly become the catalyst and tell the buyer, seller, or both what to do.

Before I tell you about this closing, there is something about selling real estate that you need to know. Back when this transaction took place, in my state, we always represented the seller not the buyer. Each state has its own laws pertaining to real estate. That has changed, and today the sales agent *usually* represents the seller, the buyer, both, or neither. It is called the "law of agency." You need to thoroughly know the requirements of your state.

The sales agent has a fiduciary relationship with the person he represents. That means the person he represents must know everything about the transaction that the sales agent knows.

Therefore, you have to remember when you are presenting the counteroffer to the person you represent, if you know something the other person is willing to do, even though it is not in the written offer or counteroffer, by law, **you must tell him**. You will understand this better after I explain this closing.

It happened that I had an offer on a property listed by another sales agent in my office. The offer was low, and the agent wanted to go along to see how I would handle it. Right away the seller countered $6,000 higher than the offer. I knew it was going to take some time, so I told both buyer and seller not to go anywhere because I would be coming back to them with counteroffers.

There were several counteroffers back and forth for an hour or so involving lots of drama. Finally we got down to a difference of $1,000. Neither buyer nor seller would budge. I was in the seller's house. I told him the buyer was standing firm on his counteroffer. He wouldn't make a counter. Therefore, the sale was finished.

The sales agent with me also thought it was finished. It would have been, except I had one ace up my sleeve. It was now time for the orchestrated close. This is where a catalyst is needed, and I was that catalyst. Remember, the catalyst makes things happen that otherwise wouldn't.

I told the seller I knew he was disappointed. Then I stood up, picked up my briefcase and moved toward the door as if I were leaving. I had no intention of leaving; however, that heightened his disappointment and completely changed his mood, knowing he was about to lose the sale.

The agent with me also stood up to leave. At the door, I stopped, turned around and started talking again. I went over and sat back down in my chair. I could tell the sales agent with me was confused, but she also sat down.

I told the seller I knew he wanted to sell, and I was just as disappointed as he was. I said, "We came so close it would be a shame to lose this sale," I said, "It may be useless, but I want to go back to the buyer one more time."

Then I said, "I am not going to ask you to make a counteroffer because I think it will be useless. However, I want you to give me one more chance. Agree to this without putting it in writing, and if by some miracle I am able to get the buyer to come up another $500, I want you to agree to accept it." After some hesitation he said he would.

At this point in the transaction, I had the written counteroffer from the buyer, but only a verbal agreement with the seller. By law I represented the seller. Therefore, I had some liberty with the buyer that I didn't have with the seller. That doesn't mean I can be dishonest, it means because he is not my client, I don't have to tell him the seller will possibly go down another $500.

I headed back to the buyer. I told him the seller would not go down another $1,000, which was true. I told him I felt like he knew all along he wouldn't go down that much. Therefore, the sale was over. I knew he was disappointed. I could see the look of disappointment on his face as I stood up to leave.

Then with a look of being deep in thought, I said, "We came so close. I hate to give up now; we are only $1,000 apart." Next, I did not ask; I told him to give me one more chance to put this deal together. I told him to raise his counteroffer by $500, and I would give it one final effort. I guaranteed him there would be no more counteroffers.

After some deep thought, he reluctantly agreed to increase his counter, and the sale was made.

I knew both buyer and seller wanted to make this sale;

that is why I was able to take control. Did you notice at the end, rather than "ask" I "told" both buyer and seller what to do, and we made the sale!

Remember, the catalyst is what causes the reaction. In this case, make the sale.

Throughout this ordeal, there was a lot of drama, stress, and tension. The agent with me did not have a clue about what was happening.

When we got into the car to leave, she told me she thought it was the worst day of her life. On the other hand, it was one of my better days. I was elated and so were both the buyer and seller.

I try to learn by reflecting and analyzing the events of my transactions. In this case, I already knew. This sale was not about the price. It was a classic case of the buyer not wanting to pay one dollar more than necessary. At the same time, the seller did not want to sell for one dollar less than necessary. That is why they were both elated.

They each knew they had gotten the very best deal possible. As for the other sales agent, she was as confused as a termite in a yo-yo and learned nothing from the experience. "Bless her Heart!"

## Important lessons in this chapter!

1. Learn to do the "Orchestrated Close." It is very effective and great fun!

2. Always remember who you represent and that you have a fiduciary relationship with them.

3. Sometimes you must tell the buyer and seller what to do.

# CHAPTER SEVENTEEN
## The "Not Worker"

Let's pause for a moment and discuss a different subject. I started to make this one of my little "Wisdom Nuggets," but because of the importance of dealing with the "Not Worker," I decided to make it a separate chapter. That is because I wanted it to stand out. This is more important than most people realize. Improper handling of the "Not Worker" can be detrimental to your career as a salesman, especially if you work in a large office.

Once I attended a seminar where I was warned about the "Not Worker." Unfortunately, they are in practically every sales organization. They are very sociable and lovable. Because they are sociable, you seldom see them alone. They love being with other people, especially other "Not Workers." By now you probably have figured out I am talking about, someone who is not working.

It may be a fellow salesperson. It could even be a relative or friend who thinks you do not have a real job, because you do not have to be at the office at a certain time. They know you can take off anytime if needed.

They do not understand you do have a real job. It is just different from the normal 8 to 5 jobs to which they are accustomed. If you pay close attention, you will discover many "Not Workers" are depressed, lonely, bored, and looking for something to do, as long as it is not working.

The "Not Worker" is often a fellow salesperson who will roam the hallway or snack area, looking for someone to talk to, or to tell the latest joke. If he approaches you and you are working, he will attempt to get you to join his club of "Not Workers." He never seems to quit.

It is impossible to avoid him. If you do not learn how

to deal with him, you may end up as a member of the "Not Worker" Club. It reminds me of a science fiction movie I once saw called the "Body Snatchers." If you hung around with those people and fell asleep, they would invade and take over your body.

In dealing with them, you don't want to be rude. Often they are very nice people. It is just that they have a problem of not working. Among their many problems, they may have financial problems which are probably caused because they are "Not Working."

They can be very depressing and can cause you to be depressed as well. You would not want to hang around with this kind of person. You may have empathy for them, but you cannot help them. Their problem is normally deep seated, and they may need professional help.

Since you cannot help them, you should try to avoid them as much as possible when you are working. If you want to try and help, do it when you also are not working. You should choose the time and place.

If you are approached by a "Not Worker" while you are working, tell him right now is not a good time. You must (fill in the blank: meet someone, make a phone call, prepare for a meeting, go to a closing, etc.). Tell him to meet you after 5, 6, or whatever time you choose.

Tell him you will be happy to hear his story, listen to his joke, give him advice, or whatever he is asking of you. Just do it when you're not working. You can say, "Maybe we can go to lunch tomorrow." You must be consistent in your persistence of avoiding him and not allowing him to abuse your time. After a while, hopefully he will give up and scout out someone who will be easier prey.

**An important lesson in this chapter!** Be busy and focus on your work. Don't let others abuse your time.

# CHAPTER EIGHTEEN
## Attitude

I will always choose someone with a "can do" attitude and mediocre talent over someone with great talent and a poor attitude. With hard work, study, and a great attitude, a person can considerably improve their talent.

In Chapter Fifteen titled: *Staying Motivated.* I talked about getting a list of the names and phone numbers of graduating high school seniors. Notice when I went back the second time my ability had not changed; my attitude did. That's why I got the list.

The Valdosta Wildcats of Valdosta, Georgia, has the record of the most wins of any high school football team in the nation. Why is that? An example is given below.

In 2016 they were playing for the state championship. The team they were playing was bigger and stronger than they. The title game was televised and played in the Georgia Dome in Atlanta, Georgia. Guess who won? More importantly, why did the Wildcats win? They were smaller, weaker, and very much the underdog.

I believe the reason is because their opponent went to the Georgia Dome to play for the state championship. But not the Wildcats, they went to the Georgia Dome to **WIN** the state championship. That is different and that is why they won. **A positive "can do" attitude will almost always win out over ability!**

So, why would you or anyone want to be an average or even a good salesman when you can be a Super Salesman? If you have the desire, a **can do** attitude, a willingness to learn, and with **the same amount of effort**, you can become a Super Salesman! Best of all, you will have fun during the process.

# CHAPTER NINETEEN
## Wisdom Nuggets

This chapter will be a "catch-all" of many of the experiences both large and small that I have encountered in my career. I will call them "Wisdom Nuggets." No one "Nugget" is large enough to write a full chapter. Therefore, I will group them all together into one chapter. That is good, because you will have one location to go to and find many of the situations and problems you will also encounter.

These "Nuggets" will not be in any certain order. It will just be a litany of problems, answers, situations, and solutions I have encountered. You can learn by seeing how these situations were handled.

I am going to start thinking and writing. Since I am reminiscing this will probably be a long chapter. That is good, because the more I remember the better for you. I hope you are looking forward to reading this chapter with as much anticipation as I have in writing it.

It would be difficult to read and remember all these nuggets. Therefore, I have a suggestion. Start with number one and write the consecutive number of each nugget on your calendar. Write one nugget for each week. It can be a reminder for you to read again and think on that particular nugget during that week.

Since there are 52, that will give you a nugget for each week in the year. In one year you will become very familiar with each of them. Do this every year as long as you are a salesman. In time it will become a part of how you think.

### *Wisdom Nugget 1: Be Reliable*

A Super Salesman has many irons in the fire at the same time. Sometimes it is difficult to keep up with everything. However, it is imperative to meet all your commitments on a timely basis.

It is absolutely necessary to become and stay organized. If humanly possible, never be late or forget an appointment. If you have to be late, call and let your customer know as soon as possible.

Are you always late? If so, pay attention! Say you were offered $700,000 to meet someone the next morning at exactly 6:51 a.m. and not one minute later. Would you be late? Would you set two, maybe three alarm clocks? Would you leave early in case something unforeseen should occur? Why would you not be late? You are always late? It's because the consequences for being late are too great. The point I'm making is this; you are always late because being on time is not a priority for you!

Perhaps you have never thought of it this way, but being late means you are rude and inconsiderate of other people's time. You need to change that attitude!

You never want to get a reputation of being unreliable. Here is one of many reasons why: Last night I was up past 2 a.m., editing this book. The next morning I got up shortly after 8 a.m. because a friend said he was coming over at 9.

You probably guessed it, he didn't show. Later that morning he called to tell me he couldn't come, because the afternoon before, he had made an appointment with the TV repairman. It would have been nice had he called the night before and I could have slept-in. You never know how much trouble being late causes others.

Never think just because you have a good excuse it's OK to be late, that is, unless you communicate it to the other person on a timely basis.

There are all kinds of electronic gadgets to assist you. Get a Smartphone; it will be invaluable in assisting you in recording your appointments and sounding an alarm to remind you in a timely manner. If you wish to become a Super Salesman remember to always consider the inconvenience you will cause if you are late or do not show up at all.

You must train yourself to immediately record appointments and other information on your phone. Also, there are contact software programs designed specifically for assisting you in staying in touch with your customers. I will have more on that in the next chapter titled: *How to Become a Super Salesman.*

## Wisdom Nugget 2:  Selling By Telling Stories

I have found that people love to hear stories. Therefore, when you tell a story, people will listen, be persuaded, and remember. You will find it is always good, if possible, to work a story into your sale. Try to make your point by telling a story. You will see I have done it throughout this book.

Here is an example. Over the years I have had sellers with all kind of reasons why they had to get a certain price for their property. One told me he was going to California, and the prices of houses are much higher out there; therefore, he had to sell for a certain price.

Another said he had paid a certain price for his home; therefore he had to sell it for more than he had paid. Never mind he had paid too much. I told the first seller I have never known of a buyer willing to pay more than market value just because the seller was moving to California. Here is how I used my "Navigator Story" to deal with the second situation.

It goes like this. Suppose you are on the east coast and go to the airport and board a plane bound for Atlanta, Georgia. After you've been flying for 45 minutes the navigator tells the pilot he is off course. He tells him he thought he said Atlantic instead of Atlanta; therefore you are flying way off course out over the Atlantic Ocean.

The pilot says he cannot turn around, because they have been flying for 45 minutes. It would waste another 45 minutes to get back on course. They cannot afford to waste that amount of time and that much fuel; therefore, they will have to continue. If they do, it is obvious they are headed for disaster.

I would then ask the seller what he would want the pilot to do. After all, they have wasted a lot of time and fuel. I have never had anyone say they would want the pilot to keep on the same course. They all wanted the pilot to turn around and get back on course immediately.

Then I say to the seller, "That is exactly your situation." Your price is way too high. Since you are off course, you must turn around immediately. I would say, "If you made a mistake by paying too much when you bought the house, it has nothing to do with what is happening now. You must get back on course."

Notice, I didn't say he paid too much, I said "if." That way, he is less likely to be offended and want to argue about whether or not he paid too much. Also, it may be that the market has dropped. It is not unusual for a property to be less valuable because of a change in market conditions.

After telling the story, if they still wanted to argue price, I would say, "We will list it at your price and test the market. We can always change course later if necessary." This Navigator story can be used in any situation when someone is off course in their thinking. Use this story, and

**think** of other stories you can use or make up to apply to your various selling situations.

### Wisdom Nugget 3:  Don't Be Timid

I sold a house to a young military couple very early in my selling career. Not long afterward, the husband got orders to be transferred. He needed to sell his house and called me to list it. I knew the price he wanted was too high.

I should have been more insistent when I told him it was too high; however, I was a little timid. I listed the house at his price and placed it on the market to sell. I should have gone back after a few weeks and told him why he should reduce his price but I didn't. After several months it didn't sell and he was down to the wire. He had to make a drastic reduction in price to sell it quickly.

He was very upset with me, because he felt I wasn't assertive enough in pointing out the importance of reducing the price sooner. Fortunately, we did sell it for a small profit. Had the price been lowered sooner, I believe his house may have sold for a higher price with a lot less stress, and he would have made more profit.

Perhaps it was because of this I became overly concerned with getting the price right before I listed a property. That involved another learning lesson which was discussed earlier in chapter 12. Those two incidents taught me how to handle an overpriced listing. Just think, you can learn it now without going through the ordeals I went through before I learned.

### Wisdom Nugget 4: The Selling Environment

When working with your customer, you should take control. If the TV is blaring, ask if they would mind turning it off? I didn't say turn down the volume. Tell them you may be distracted and forget to tell them something important.

Do not say it may distract them. You are taking the blame by saying it could distract you. If you do not do this, the customer may try to listen to you and watch the TV at the same time. One way to avoid this is to sit in the dining room and not the living room.

Next, you should suggest the seating arrangement. If it is a couple, you do not want them facing each other. They could be making gestures to one another, and you wouldn't know it.

You want them to be facing you. That way you can see by their facial expressions if they are getting the points you are making. You could arrange the seating any way you or they like as long as they are both facing you.

### Wisdom Nugget 5: "Outside The Box" Again

In an earlier chapter I talked about working "outside the box." Here is another example. You may think it most unusual the way I handled this type situation. I feel sure most salesmen would think it extremely unorthodox. I knew I was taking a risk to do it; however, in all my years of selling, I never lost a buyer when I did this. While showing houses to a buyer, sometimes I would drive by a house that had the owner's for sale sign in their yard.

If I noticed the buyer was paying particular attention to the house, I would ask if they would like to see it. My thinking was the buyer would probably go back to the house as soon as I let them out of my car. Therefore, by doing it this way, I would still be involved with the buyers. If I noticed something detrimental about the house I could bring it to their attention.

If they wanted to see it, I would park the car in the driveway and walk up to the front door and ring the doorbell. Note: I left my customer in the car. According to whether it was summer or winter, I would leave the air conditioner or heater on and the windows rolled up. I did not want them to hear me negotiate.

When the owner came to the door, I asked the price of their home. I asked if I sold it for the price they were asking, would they pay me a commission? I wouldn't add my commission and quote a higher price to the buyer. That was because if they found out and they probably would, I would lose credibility.

Sometimes the owner said, "Yes." Sometimes we would negotiate the commission rate on the spot. If they said, "No," I asked if they would mind if I sat on the couch while they showed the home to my customer. I told them I would come back later to let them know what my customer had to say about their home.

The owner would take the buyer into the kitchen and say, "This is the kitchen" or into the bedroom and say, "This is the bedroom" followed by a long pause. This would go on throughout the house. It was obvious the owner did not know how to sell. Sometimes it was even humorous.

As soon as we finished looking at houses, I would go back to the homeowner to give a report of what my buyer thought of their home. In situations like this often I ended up listing their house, because the owner knew I had buyers.

It never happened, but if my buyer had bought the house directly from the owner without me being involved, perhaps I could offer assistance and guidance for a reduced commission. In addition, I believe both owner and buyer may have felt badly for me. Hopefully they would feel obligated to help me find another buyer as a replacement. This could translate into many buying and selling referrals in the future. It could be a win-win situation for everyone.

### *Wisdom Nugget 6:  Presentation Book*

Early in my selling career, I developed a presentation book for listing properties. It was very effective. Such a book will keep you from rambling. It will help you to know how long it will take to make your listing presentation. It will keep you on tract so you don't leave out anything you wanted to say. You also could make one! Any pictures or writing in it should be very large and not very busy.

I had a picture in mine of two rough looking characters on either side of a large dollar bill, pulling like in a "tug of war." Under the picture of one person, I had the word *buyer* and under the other was the word *seller*. I used it to show there is always a conflict between buyers and sellers. That is because their interest is in direct opposition to one another. The book helped to remind me to tell sellers of why they needed a professional salesperson to represent them.

On one page I had a picture of a bee collecting nectar from a flower. I explained the many ways a seller could get stung by not using a professional.

I would say: "It is like trying to get honey from the beehive, instead of the store. There is a small possibility you could save some money, but the chances are greater you will get stung." I then went on to tell them many of the problems that can and do happen between buyers and sellers.

An easy and very inexpensive way to make the book is to go to a website named "FIVERR." You can find someone on that site to do illustrations and help you develop your book. You could develop the book to cover the points you want to use in your listing presentation.

In the back of the book you could have a list of every property by address that you have ever listed and sold. Remember if you list a property and it sells, even by another agent, you can take credit for the sale. That is because you were a part of it. Also, you could have a list of handwritten and typed testimonials from your many past satisfied customers.

### Wisdom Nugget 7:  Use Persuasion Not Force

Remember you are a salesman. It matters not whether you are selling a product or if it is life in general. It is better to get your way by persuasion, not by force. After I had been in the real estate business for a number of years, I became an owner and broker of a medium size company. I continued to sell, because I did not want to be out of touch with the problems of my agents. Naturally, all their problems would come to me and become my problem.

One day one of my agents came into my office and said she had an irate builder in her office. He wanted to cancel all his listings. He was going to take them to another company. When I stepped into her office, he was furious. It appeared he was almost ready to hit someone. He wanted his listings and my agent had told him the listings did not expire until sometime in the not too distant future. That was easy for me to handle. All I had to do was to disarm him.

I told him, "If you're not happy with our service, we will not hold you to the contracts against your will." He said **"Really?!"** I then handed him the folder with his listing contracts. I told him we would cancel them, and he could immediately walk out the door with them after I made copies for my record.

It was amazing how fast his mood changed. He became more relaxed and friendly. You cannot sell when a person is emotional. Then I started selling. I found out what his complaint was. I sold him on why he should leave the listings with us. He was very happy when he left. We were also happy, because he left the listings with us.

After he left, I told my agent she had backed him into a corner by telling him the listings had not yet expired. I further told her no one likes to be backed into a corner. If they are, they will come out fighting almost every time. I told her, "You are a salesperson, so use persuasion instead of force."

Understand, you must move your customer from emotion to logic before you can start selling. There may come a time when force would have to be used. If so, it should be only in extremely important critical situations and the very last alternative.

### Wisdom Nugget 8: What You Don't Know

When I retired from the Air Force, the Veterans Administration had a policy of allowing veterans to use civilian dentists to do whatever was necessary to put their teeth in good order without any cost to the veteran. This was allowed only during the first year after retiring. A retired veteran could get crowns, caps, fillings, or anything else to put their teeth and mouth in good condition. Obviously, I picked the dentist who I was told was the best in town.

The dentist had to do extensive work requiring several crowns, and it took many appointments over a period of about three months. Toward the end of my appointments he told me he was going to sell his house, because he was building a new home out on his farm. He wanted to list the old house with me but only for 30 days.

He said he needed to sell immediately, because his new home was almost completely built. I thought the price he wanted was way higher than market value. I told him I thought his price was too high, especially to sell it so quickly.

During our discussion, he told me he had another patient who was a real estate agent, and he owed him a favor. He said, "Since you think my price is too high, would you mind if I list it with the other agent for 30 days? If it doesn't sell, I will list it with you." I was relieved and thrilled. I thought after 30 days he would be willing to adjust to a more realistic price.

This was the beginning of my learning you don't know what you don't know. It took me a couple of lessons to learn, but I did learn. What I didn't know is this. There was a man in our area who had said if that house ever comes on the market to sale, he wanted to buy it.

He did buy it, and I lost what could have been an easy sale. By learning the "how to" of selling taught in this book, hopefully you can learn these lessons, and it won't cost you like it did me.

### Wisdom Nugget 9: The Recreational Buyer

Be aware that some potential buyers look at houses for fun or because they have nothing better to do. More than once I have had a retired couple who were just traveling around the country looking at houses. I call them recreational buyers. That is because that is how they entertain themselves. Find out if they are recreational buyers by paying attention, listening, asking questions, and thinking.

You want to know if you have a potential buyer before you waste a day or two of your time. Some buyers do not realize you are working a real job. They think you are socializing with them. If you let them, they will waste a lot of your time. You have to be careful how you handle them, because later they may become real buyers.

A potential buyer may decide to upgrade to a larger house or downgrade to a smaller one. If this buyer is a retired couple or if one or both of the partners are not working, they may want to immediately start looking for a house to buy. In most cases, if they found a house and fell in love with it today, they could not place an offer on it until their house sells. In the meantime the house they want may sell while they are waiting for theirs to sell.

Tell them when their house sells you will work diligently and quickly with them to find a home. Then when they find it, they will be able to make an offer. If they have not yet listed their home with you, let them know it is important to list it immediately.

The sooner it sells the sooner they can start looking for a replacement home. If they insist on looking at houses now and some customers will, as a last resort, give them a list of houses and send them out to look on their own. Let them know your time could be used more effectively in trying to sell their house.

Now for a note of caution: it is risky to send a potential buyer out on their own, because another agent could intercept them. That is why it is important to have their house listed immediately. That will help you to retain control and a close relationship with the buyer.

### Wisdom Nugget 10: The "Blabber Mouth"

When I was in the military, I had a "SECRET" clearance. That meant I could view any document with a Secret or lesser classification. However, I could not view the document unless I had a "need to know." Now, let's apply that to selling real estate. When you are working on any transaction, others around you do not have a "need to know" on what you are working.

Sometimes you may be working on making an offer on a property that is listed with another agent. That agent may or may not have a "need to know," according to the circumstances. Therefore, he is the only one you should have any discussion with concerning the sale of that property.

I could tell you numerous sad stories about an agent who lost a sale or caused hard feelings, because he would get excited and let everyone know on what he was working, me included. If you are a "Blabber Mouth," it will come back to haunt you.

I have already given one example of this in Chapter 9. Here is another of many, many examples I could give. Every Wednesday morning, most of the sales agents in our company would load up in cars and view houses that had just been listed. We called it "caravanning."

Early in my career while caravanning, I looked at a house and blurted out, "This is just the house for my customer." I figured I would have this sale wrapped up by early afternoon.

It turned out that another agent was working with a customer on the same house. He told me he was planning to place an offer on it that night, so he wanted me to back off until after he presented his offer.

Now what do I do? If I proceed, it will cause hard feelings with that agent. If I don't proceed, it will not be fair to my customer or the seller of the house, because his deal might not go through, plus I could lose a commission. This wouldn't have been an issue if I had kept my mouth shut.

Often, a sales agent has intentions of trying to list or sell a particular property. However, it may not be a top priority, that is until he finds out someone else is attempting to list or sell the same property. Early in my sales career, I decided never to give my fellow agents an advantage by telling them on what I was working.

If a sales agent told me he was working on a certain property, it would give me an advantage. However, if I hadn't asked for the information, I saw no reason to stop what I was doing even if I was working on the same property.

Be very careful how you handle these situations. If it becomes your philosophy never to discuss on what you are working, do not broadcast it. You don't want to become known as secretive. If you do, other agents may also think you are sneaky.

### Wisdom Nugget 11: Going the Extra Mile

Because I drove many miles to hold this sale together, I am going to change the old saying of "going the extra mile," to "going the extra miles." One Saturday morning, a friend of mine who owned a large new car dealership called and asked me to meet him. He introduced me to his new sales manager and wife. His manager was moving to Valdosta, Georgia, from Macon, Georgia, about 160 miles north of Valdosta. My friend wanted me to help them find a new home to buy.

The sales manager, his wife, and I spent the rest of that Saturday looking at houses. Late in the afternoon, we found the perfect home. It was somewhat expensive; however because the manager was getting a large pay increase in his new job, he decided he could afford it. Before we could get the paperwork done, they had to return to Macon. We set up a time for me to call the next day to go over the sales documents.

When I called early the next afternoon, he said something during our conversation that made me think there might be a problem. It made me nervous. This represented a big sale for me, and I didn't want to lose it.

I decided since it was a Sunday afternoon and I had some free time, I would drive to Macon. I decided to go even though it was a two and a half hour drive one way. I didn't want to call him, because he may tell me not to come. This was before we had cell phones, so I asked my wife to call after I left and let him know I was coming.

Sure enough when I arrived, I discovered there was a big problem. His wife was pregnant with their first child and hadn't told him until they got back home. Knowing she would be out of work for a long time, he was afraid they couldn't afford the house. After some discussion, I could tell he was reluctant, but he signed the offer, and I happily drove the two and a half hours back home. They closed out the house and were very happy with the decision they made.

Several months later he told me he wouldn't have bought the house had I not driven all the way to Macon. He said he could not believe I would drive that distance just to help him get the home. He said after I drove that far, he didn't have the heart not sign the contract.

## Wisdom Nugget 12:  Contact Program

I will write more about contact program software in the last chapter titled: *How to Become a Super Salesman*. For now, let me just say, "Get a contact program and use it." In the last chapter I will tell how Stanley Mills, a real Super Salesman, used his. It helped him to stay in contact with all his many customers and prospects. You can find a program designed specifically for the real estate industry. They are available for many other professions as well.

If you cannot find one that suits you, pay a few dollars to someone to modify an accounting program just for your requirements. Once you get a program, spend the time needed to learn how to use all its features.

It will be an invaluable help to you. Do this in the very beginning of your sales career, not later when you are well on the road to becoming a Super Salesman. It will help you get there sooner. A contact program will be a major factor in assisting you in reaching that lofty goal.

Technology is continually evolving. It is changing the way we work, live, and play. We didn't have many of the gadgets of today when I started my sales career. First we got beepers, next it was computers, then cell phones. In the beginning, many sales agents refused to learn how to email, scan, text, or use the new technologies of the day. Obviously, those agents were left far behind their competitors.

The pace of change is accelerating. Cars are beginning to drive themselves. Three-D printers are printing body parts, airplane parts, and houses. Even our money system is evolving with crypto/digital currency. If you want to be a Super Salesman, embrace technology. Take the time to learn how technology can help you advance your selling career at a more rapid pace.

### Wisdom Nugget 13: Success Breeds Success

Choose your friends and acquaintances very carefully. You can divide people into two categories. One is the happy, positive, optimistic, and always a smile on their face type person. These are the people you and others enjoy. Your job as a salesman will be much easier if you associate with these kinds of people.

The other type person is the negative, pessimistic, doom, and gloom person. They seem to have been born in the objective mood. They love to tell a story as long as it is negative. Avoid them! They will pull you down to their level. You will learn nothing beneficial from them. It is easy to become like the people with whom you associate.

You need to surround yourself with people who will encourage you and help you brainstorm. You want to become more like them. Success breeds success and negativity breeds negativity.

### Wisdom Nugget 14:  A lesson In Humility

Even today after all these years, I am embarrassed as I write about this lesson I learned at the beginning of my real estate career. Thankfully it was in the beginning and not at the end. In the first few months of my selling career all our sales agents went on a caravan to a small mobile home.

A mobile home is personal property; therefore, we don't sell them unless the land is included in the sale. As I walked through it, I thought it was a dump. I knew I wouldn't be showing it, because who would buy and live in such a place. Late that afternoon, a man I knew called me. So no one will recognize who he is, I will call him Jim.

Jim had very little formal education. He was a common laborer. He would do odd jobs, but mainly he was a painter. He lived in the area where the mobile home was located. He had ridden by it and saw the for sale sign. He wanted me to show it to him.

He and his wife "oohed and aahed" over it like it was the Taj Mahal. It made me realize that everyone is not as blessed mentally and financially as I am. It made me to be more appreciative and thankful for what I have. It also taught me not to make judgments about what other people would want.

### Wisdom Nugget 15: Making Judgments

Throughout this book I have examples of making judgments and misjudgments. The Wisdom Nugget you just read is an example. Still, there are times we have to make judgments. Someone once said prejudging without investigation is the height of ignorance.

Therefore, always be aware that you may not have all the facts. Earlier I made the statement, "You don't know what you don't know."

Once I had a new neighbor who bought the house across the street from me. When we met, the first thing he told me was he knew he had paid too much for his home. I didn't mention anything about the price he had paid, so someone must have already told him he had paid too much.

He explained that he had five children all under the age of ten. He said he paid too much for the house, because it had a large room above the garage. The ceiling in the room was only six feet high. It was unsuitable for adults but ideal for kids. So he converted it into a playroom. He said he could put all his kids up there and know they were safe.

He said he had sold his home in New Jersey for considerably more than he had paid for this house. That was why he was willing to pay more than the house was worth.

Try to be less judgmental until you know all the facts. Since you will probably never know all the facts, do not presume you know what a customer will or will not do. Your misjudgments could cause you to miss listing a property or making a sale.

### Wisdom Nugget 16: Above the Competition

Once I had a customer complain about one of my sales agents. This agent was attempting to list their home. He told the customer his price was too high. The customer asked me, "How would he know; he didn't even look at the house?"

Never let that happen to you. Always look, sound, and act professional. It is not always necessary to wear a suit and tie; however, you should always be neat, clean, and well groomed.

I always encouraged the customer to show me their home. I wanted them to be with me to see what I was doing. I would have a miniature tape recorder. I used it to record comments as I would view the home. I seldom, if ever, had to refer back to it. However, it was available if I ever needed it.

I took along an electronic measuring device to measure rooms. I didn't measure the whole house; however, I would find an excuse to measure at least one room. All I had to do to get a measurement was to point and press a button. It was very impressive. The main reason I did this was to let the customer know I embraced and used technology.

Another thing I always did was look into the attic and comment about whether the roof was stick built or built using trusses. I would say something about their gable or hip roof. That was to impress the customer with the fact that I knew something about building houses. It helped me to be a cut above my competition. You can use these ideas or develop your own.

### Wisdom Nugget 17: Extrovert vs Introvert

Which personality type do you suppose makes the best salesman? The extrovert is outgoing, friendly, sometimes loud, and is a people person. Usually people like to be around that type person. However, sometimes they are talking when they should be listening.

The introvert tends to listen more and is reflective. However, they do not always give the impression of being very friendly.

Both types can make a Super Salesman. You may be surprised to learn that it is my opinion the Introvert by far tends to make the best salesman. The reason is they listen more and are more thoughtful and reflective.

In the next chapter I talk about "conditioning." Normally when we think of conditioning, it is negative conditioning. Fortunately, we humans have intellect, and we can consciously condition ourselves in positive ways.

That means, in a selling situation, the extrovert can condition himself to tone things down and force himself to think and be more reflective. The introvert can condition himself to be more friendly and outgoing.

Over time, both types will become more comfortable with these small tweaks they consciously make to their personalities. These changes can then become a part of their personality. Thus, they will move closer to the middle becoming an ambivert. Think about this when you read about conditioning and goal setting in the next chapter.

### Wisdom Nugget 18: Conventions & Seminars

If the company you work for is a member of a national franchise, you can take advantage of what they have to offer. Most will have annual conventions for their members.

The National Associations of REALTORS® and the state associations affiliated with them have conventions. Attend as many of them as you can. Do this especially in the beginning of your sales career.

This is not a vacation. You should be doing a considerable amount of work during the day, as well as at night. These conventions will have many workshops. There will probably be so many you will not be able to attend them all.

Pick the ones that interest you or are in areas where you are weak. Especially, attend any computer workshop so you can keep abreast of new technology.

Take hundreds of your business cards with you. Give them to all the attendees you meet. Also, get as many cards as possible from other attendees.

You want to build a network of sales people throughout the nation. When you or they, have customers moving from one location to another, you want to get or give a referral fee. The referral fee is most often overlooked, but it should not be. It is like the icing on a cake.

Think of it as if you were buying a suit. A good salesman will sell you a shirt and tie plus a pair of socks to go with it. In the evening your day is not yet done. You should still be working.

Go to dinner with your fellow agents. Select the high producers. Pick their brain. You are trying to learn as much as possible. If you get one good idea or suggestion, it will pay for the trip and make it all worthwhile.

The same thing applies in attending seminars. Often your state or local board will have seminars or workshops. Be sure to attend them. Some of the most important lessons I learned was in a seminar or workshop.

### Wisdom Nugget 19: Promote Yourself

You want to be known in your community, so take advantage of free local advertising. There are many ways to do this. You can have your own personal magazine. That is discussed in the next chapter.

You can write articles to the editor of your local newspaper. You can ask them about writing a weekly news or informative article about real estate. They will often run it free. Look on the INTERNET; for a small fee, there are services that will provide you with print ready articles which you can change and personalize. Be careful not to be controversial.

Your car can be a great source of free advertising. Have magnetic signs made and place them on your car. They should not be "busy." I recommend that you not even list your phone number on them. Most people will not write it down especially if your car is moving. You just want everyone to think of you and your company when they are buying or selling their property.

That is the way Coca-Cola® advertises. When you get thirsty, they want you to think of coke. Print your name **large** and **bold**. Unless an address is required by law or your company requires it, you should print the name of your company without the address.

My signs and business cards were red and blue. When placed on a white background, I had three colors for the price of two. Don't ever take these signs off your automobile, except for two reasons.

One reason is when you wash your car. The other reason is when you list a house. Sometimes you may have a hard sale and have to come back later to finish listing the property.

You don't want your competitors to see your car and know you are working on a listing. Especially, you do not want them to know a property is available for listing. Oops, there is a third reason to remove the signs. It is when you sell your car.

I have known of sales agents who would take the signs off their car when they went to church. I was one of them. That all changed when someone that sat on the other end of my pew listed their house to sell with a sales agent in another company.

They were so apologetic when they found out I sold

real estate. There is no reason to feel guilty, because the signs are on your car. That is unless the only reason you go to church is to get customers.

Join a local civic club. The members of the club are potential buyers and sellers. In addition, you can make speeches at other local civic clubs. However, many people are very fearful of making a speech. One of the best ways to overcome that is to know your subject matter extremely well.

Study the subject and practice out loud in front of a mirror or video it. If you do not know how to make a speech, join the local Toastmasters Club. They will teach you and give you opportunities to practice.

Remember, many of their members will be buying and selling properties from time to time. I will have more to say on this in Wisdom Nugget 35 on facing your fears.

## *Wisdom Nugget 20: See the People*

Over the years, I have read many motivational stories. Others I have heard on CDs, tapes, and even the radio. I do not remember where I heard this story, but it had a lasting impact on me, because I knew the message was true. Here's the story.

Long after the great author, motivator, and salesman, Napoleon Hill had retired he was hired to give the keynote address at a large national sales convention. There were thousands of salesmen present.

Many made a special effort to attend because they were told Napoleon Hill was giving the keynote address. He was going to give them the secret to making huge increases in their sales. Napoleon was flown in and paid thousands of dollars to make the speech.

During the several days of the convention, the anticipation was as if electricity was in the air. Then on the final day it was time for the keynote address.

Napoleon came to the podium, old, gray-haired, and bent. He announced that he was hired to tell all the salesmen how to make large increases in their sales. Next, he said, **"See the People!... See the People!... See the People!..."** He then turned and walked off the stage.

What a letdown! Three words, said three times with a long pause between each statement. That was it. It was a great disappointment to everyone. However, years later the Super Salesmen who emerged from that crowd said it was the greatest advice they had ever received.

Almost everyone stated of all the seminars, workshops, and conventions they had ever attended, none remembered the advice like the advice that Napoleon had given that day. Even today, after all these years, we are still talking about it.

### Wisdom Nugget 21: Think Before You Answer

If someone says something in a very stern voice with a frown on their face, a person may react in a negative way. On the other hand, if it is said in a very gentle and mellow voice with a smile, chances are the reaction will be positive. If you have something negative to say, think about how you are going to say it and what the reaction will be from the person to whom you are speaking.

Here is an example. Shortly after I joined the U. S. Air Force, I decided to get a part-time job selling mutual funds. The job only lasted a short time. It ended when I was transferred to the Philippine Islands.

At the time, my older brother was an insurance salesman. He told me of a woman whose husband had recently died, and she received some money from an insurance policy. She wanted to invest it but did not know where or how.

He set up the appointment and went with me for my presentation. I thought I was doing an outstanding job, and she seemed interested. Towards the end of my presentation, she asked if she could lose any of her money. Wanting to be very honest, I told her she could "lose every dime."

Then, I pointed out why that wouldn't happen. I asked her if she thought kids would stop riding bicycles. I asked if she thought people would stop buying furniture, cars, houses, food, clothes, etc.

Every time she said, "No." I told her she was right, people will always buy those things. Therefore, it made sense to invest in the companies that make them. I was on a roll and thought I was going to make a sale.

When we got into the car to go home, my brother started laughing. He said I had done an excellent job of selling her by asking all the questions about people buying bicycles, cars, furniture, food, etc. He then said, "She is not going to buy."

I was surprised and asked him how he knew that? He said, "When you told her she could 'lose every dime,' she didn't hear another word you said after that." Sure enough, she didn't buy.

Instead of answering immediately in such a direct way, I could have answered her question with a question. I could have started asking my questions about people buying bicycles, cars, furniture, etc.

Then I could have pointed out that she could put enough money into a savings account today to buy a Honda automobile. After 20 years, when she withdraws her money from the bank, it would be the same dollar amount and even more because of interest.

However, after 20 years, the price of cars will have increased. Instead of buying a car, that amount of money may only buy a Honda motorcycle. I could have pointed out that even though she still has the money, it had lost buying power. So yes, there are risks with everything we do in life, even if we do nothing.

Be honest but think and remember, sometimes it is what you say and other times it is how you say it.

### Wisdom Nugget 22: Health Matters

Think of health like a three-legged stool. Take off one of the legs and the stool will fall. The first leg is nutrition. Your body and mind cannot function efficiently unless it is properly fed.

Too many sales agents grab a burger on the run when they can squeeze it in or just go without eating. Your body will not tolerate that over a lifetime. Therefore, you are heading for trouble.

The next leg of the stool is exercise. Never ever say you don't have enough time. The truth of the matter is we all have the same amount of time. What we are talking about is priorities.

It is imperative to get your priorities in order. Join a gym and go on a regular basis. Do not be surprised if you end up finding a customer at the gym who wants to buy or sell a house.

The last leg of the stool is rest. Get the proper amount of rest every night. You must rest your mind as well as your body. That includes taking a vacation, playing golf, going fishing, or hunting. Do whatever it is you enjoy, and don't forget to take care of the spiritual part of your life. Remember the old adage, *all work and no play makes Jack a dull boy.* You must absolutely make and take time for your health. If you lose it, nothing else in this book matters.

I have seen many salesmen who have given their

health a low priority. That is understandable. There is always a phone call to make or receive. There is always another customer to show houses or list their house.

In the real estate business, as well as most sales businesses, people constantly make demands of your time. You must take matters into your own hands and control your time.

It is a matter of priority. If it is time to eat, you should eat. If it is time to sleep, you should sleep. If it is time for exercise, you should exercise. If it is time to go to church, go to church. Yes, even if it is time to play, go play. That phone call or customer can wait.

Remember, you and only you are in control of your time. If you do not have time for your health you can and will get sick! Then, who is going to do all of those things that were so important?

Let me give you an example of how you can take control and not let others abuse your time. I had a sister-in-law who no one wanted to visit. She was elderly and lived alone. It was obvious she was lonely. That was years ago and bless her heart, she has now gone on to glory.

The reason no one wanted to visit her was because it was almost impossible to get away from her. She talked non-stop. I think she thought if she quit talking you may get a chance to say you had to leave.

When I was an Air Force Recruiter, my office was only about a block from where she worked. She was a clerk in the lobby of a large hotel. At least once or twice a week on my lunch break, I would go by and see her. She was always happy to see me and would catch me up on all the news and gossip.

After about 10 minutes of listening to her constantly talking, I would interrupt and say I had to go. She would invariably say, "Wait; let me tell you..." I would say,

"Sorry, Hazel, I have to go; tell me next time." She would follow me out the door and sometimes even down the sidewalk for a short distance. She would keep talking, and I would keep walking.

My wife said it was rude to walk off like that but it wasn't. I was the only one who would go by to see her. I did it every week, and every time the family had a reunion, she would complain to everyone. She said I was the only one in the family that would go by and visit her. It was obvious I was her favorite.

### Wisdom Nugget 23: Manage Your Investments

There will always be a demand for good salesmen. You can sell any product and work for almost any company you desire. However, one good reason for selling real estate is because you will see opportunities to make good investments.

Often those investments are income producing rental houses. Good bargains may come along because of a divorce, death, or when someone transfers and cannot sell their house prior to moving. They can't always afford to make two house payments. Therefore, they will make a substantial reduction in their price to sell it quickly.

Here is an example of why real estate can be such a great investment. Suppose you buy a rental house for $10,000 or more below market value. Let's say you pay $70,000 for it. Suppose the terms are $4,000 down and you assume the $66,000 loan and payments.

Because you bought it for $10,000 below market value, you now own an $80,000 rental property. If you do not have the time or temperament to be a Landlord, turn it over to a property management company.

Many good things can happen if you get a good tenant; just like many bad things can happen if you get a bad one. You will get a tax break by depreciating the property. Your tenant will pay for your house over time. Inflation tends to increase the value of the house. Your small $4,000 investment is now commanding a much larger investment.

By that, I mean if over a period of four or five years the property value increases by 10%, your property has increased in value by $8,000. The inflation increase is on the $80,000 value of the house, not the $4,000 investment you made as a down payment.

Of course, there is also a downside. You will have to pay insurance and property taxes, but even that is tax deductible. In addition, you will have to pay for repairs, also tax deductible.

What happens if you get a bad tenant? First of all, try not to get a bad one. You should check the tenant's credit with a credit bureau to see if they pay their bills on time.

Make inquiries of where they lived in the past and how long they lived there and did they pay their rent on time? After all that, you may still get a bad tenant. When that happens, you want to get rid of them as quickly as possible.

If you manage the property yourself, you should go over your expectations with the tenants before they move into your house. Explain that you depend upon their rent to make the payment on the house. Let them know the procedure you will use.

For instance, tell them the rent is due on the first or whatever date you choose. If you have a grace period, tell them the rent is still due on the due date, However, you will not charge them a late charge or evict them until after the grace period.

If they are late, you should immediately start the eviction process so you can evict at the end of the grace period. The first step is to send them a letter that says to pay within three days or move immediately. Each state has its own requirements. In my state, a person cannot be evicted until you send them a letter saying to pay within three days or they will be evicted.

Here is what you often run into with a bad tenant. They will make their financial problems your problem if you let them. Say the transmission on their car needs to be repaired. That is a big problem for them. They will take your rent money and get it fixed.

Now they don't have a problem. They just shifted their problem over to you. Now you have a problem. You must manage your investments, or they will manage you.

I told one tenant it looked as though he would have to move into his car, because he was not going to live in my house without paying rent. I even had one tenant say they had to go to their grandma's funeral in another state.

They forgot they used that excuse the prior year. I asked, "How many times is your grandma going to die?"

Another tenant said she could not pay her rent nor could she afford to move. She said, "I guess I'm just stuck here." After I explained the eviction process about moving her belongings out of the house onto the curb, she moved right away.

Today many people have a sense of entitlement. They have taken the "pursuit" out of "the pursuit of happiness." They think they are entitled to happiness and will take it even if it is at your expense.

Having said all that, sometimes a person may be a good tenant, but for some reason, a temporary situation has arisen, and they cannot pay the rent. Even with them, if you offer leniency, send the three-day notice so that you will be able to evict on a moments notice if it comes to that.

One last word, I have found if you forgive a late charge even once, it can start a trend. I recommend you collect the late charge in every instance. I know that sounds harsh, but it lets the tenant know where they stand right from the beginning. It can save you lots of trouble later.

## Wisdom Nugget 24: Safety

In the world we live in today, safety is a major concern. In selling real estate you are sometimes out late at night. There will be times you may be in an area where you do not feel safe. There can be danger to both male and female agents, but it is more dangerous for women. Since I am not the professional in this area, find someone who is.

You may start with the local sheriff or police departments. You can attend a safety workshop or seminar. Sometimes your local real estate board, state associations, or national association will have training seminars. Whatever advice they give, take it seriously to keep safe.

If it is lawful in your state and you decide to carry a weapon, get a concealed carry permit. In addition, join an association such as *Texas Law Shield®*. Join it so that you can buy their weapon carry insurance. **Never carry a weapon without insurance**, it is not that expensive!

## Wisdom Nugget 25: Business Cards

Do you know what most people do with business cards? They throw them into the trash. That being the case, you need to come up with an idea to make the customer or prospect want to keep your card. Here is what I did. On the next page, you will see what I had printed on the back of my cards.

You are welcome to use it if you wish. There are no copyright issues. I made it up myself. Read the instructions above the smallest box below, which is inside the larger box. Then do exactly as instructed. There are no tricks. How many F's did you count?

Overlooking the obvious in Real Estate Values? Read the sentence in the small box below, ↓ then carefully count the Fs

DETERMINING FAIR AND FULL REAL ESTATE VALUES ARE THE RESULT OF YEARS OF SCIENTIFIC STUDY COMBINED WITH MANY YEARS OF EXPERIENCE.

Count the Fs only once. You are overlooking the obvious if you did not count 6 Fs. You may also be overlooking obvious benefits and values in real estate ownership.

**HOOT GIBSON**                                    **Ph. 229 247-xxxx**

**Email: xxxxx@sssss**                          **Cell 229 247-xxxx**

Most people come up with three Fs. I have even had people place their finger on each word and stop on each letter and still come up with only three. I have seen others count four or five, then on a recount, they could only see three. Some have wanted to bet me $10 there is less than six until I explain why I think most people only see three Fs.

Do not read any further until you count the letters to see how many Fs you count!

o-o-o-o-o-o-o-o-o-o-o-o-o-o-o-o-o-o-o-o-o-o-o-o-o-o-o

If you are a skilled typist you will understand. You type the word "the" as a word, not the letters "t," "h," and "e." You think and type the word without seeing the individual letters. Notice the word "of" is used three times in the box. You see it as a word, not the individual letters, which is pronounced "ov."

Apparently the mind has an auto correct and sees the F as a V. Therefore most people miss those three Fs and see them as Vs. At least, that is what I think happens.

When one person finally saw it, he said, "I am going to keep this card and win my beer drinking money with it." By the way, if you get all six, do not brag about it. It could mean that you are not a very good reader, seeing letters instead of words. LOL

## Wisdom Nugget 26: Never Confuse "High Noon"

Contracts usually have a time for acceptance. Never use 12 a.m. or 12 p.m. for the time. Sometimes your customers will not be sure if it means 12 noon or 12 midnight. If you want to use noon or midnight as your time, do it for one minute less. Make the time of acceptance 11:59 p.m., or 11:59 a.m. That way there should never a chance for misunderstanding.

## Wisdom Nugget 27: The Bearer Of Bad News

This is definitely an area you can learn to the point it will instinctively become a part of how you think. First of all, seldom if ever, should blame be placed on the customer, even in little things.

An example of that is in Wisdom Nugget 4. If you recall, you asked the customer to turn off their TV. You told them it may distract you. What you were really thinking is it would distract them, but you didn't say that. You told the customer their TV may distract "you" and you might leave out something important.

When I give someone my phone number, I don't ask if they understand. I always ask them to repeat it to make sure "I" said the number clearly. In little things like that you can be the culprit. However, as a matter of policy, it is not wise to always be the bad guy.

You may recall one time I said when a seller's house was viewed by buyers, **they** thought the price was too high. I also said when other sales agents viewed the house

**they** thought the price was too high.

Always think of ways to let someone else give or be responsible for bad news. By that, I don't mean to never accept responsibility for your mistakes or wrong doings. What I am saying is, let someone else be the bearer of bad news.

### Wisdom Nugget 28: Prepare the house To sell

Often when you list a house to sell, it will need to be prepared to sell. You need to insist that excess furniture be removed. If the homeowner is going to give anything away, tell them to do it now.

Excess items in closets should be removed, even if they have to be placed into the attic or the basement. Any and all clutter should be removed to make the rooms and closets appear to be larger.

Animals could be placed in a kennel, with a friend, or at least outside the house. Window drapes or blinds should be open and all lights turned on and left on while showing the house.

When you begin selling houses, some of the more experienced agents you will be working with can give you more up to date information about what you need to do in preparing the house to sell. I will not elaborate on it here. Just be aware that it is necessary and important. Next is a short story about one of my experiences. It emphasizes the need to have animals removed from the house before showing.

I listed a house where the owners had a medium size, vicious, and very anxious inside dog. The reason I said anxious is because it appeared he was anxious to get hold of my leg and gnaw on it.

They had to hold the dog while I listed the house. He was barking, snarling, growling, and tugging at the leash to get to me. It was difficult to talk over the commotion, plus I was also very anxious and nervous about the dog pulling away from the owner.

The owners both worked and left the dog free to roam around in the house while they were gone. I suggested they board or leave him with a friend until the house sold. However, they said, "No, just call and we will come home and take the dog outside while the house is being shown."

About a month later, I was in the area showing houses and decided to show that particular house. However, I forgot about the dog, **not good!** I bet you know where this is heading. We went inside the house, and I walked with my customer throughout the house. As we were getting into the car to leave, I remembered the dog.

Normally, I let "sleeping dogs lie," but my curiosity got the better of me. So I decided to go back in and see where the dog was. The couch was about eight inches from the wall. When I looked behind it, I had to laugh.

There he was, as quiet as he could be. That brave vicious dog was shivering and shaking like someone had thrown a bucket of ice water on him. He was absolutely scared bark-less. I thought it was just too funny.

On a more serious note, that is something I should not have forgotten. I should have made a note on the listing sheet in a prominent place, **in bold letters,** so it would have reminded anyone who showed the house. Had the dog actually been as mean as he acted and a larger dog that wasn't a scaredy-cat, the outcome could have been much different.

### Wisdom Nugget 29: Know Your Percentages

Keep up with your success rate. If you talked to six people about buying, how many did you sell? If you talk to ten people trying to make an appointment, how many appointments did you make? Out of ten attempts to list houses, how many did you list?

Keep up with whatever you are attempting to do. By knowing your percentages, you will know the areas where you are weak and need to improve.

### Wisdom Nugget 30:  Always Be Ready

In an earlier chapter, I said to have fill in the blank forms with you at all times. That is so you will be ready to conduct business at anytime and anyplace. Now for a short story to emphasize why it is so important to be ready to do business at all times. There are many stories like this I could tell.

I knew both these individuals well. It happened one Saturday morning. A real estate agent saw a competitor sales agent leaving a house about four houses down from where he lived.

This agent had recently moved into that neighborhood and was just starting out in real estate sales. He didn't want a competitor company with a "for sale" sign a few doors down from his home.

When he saw the agent drive off, he walked down and asked his neighbor if they were thinking of selling their home. The neighbor answered, "Yes" and further stated that another agent had just left to go to his office to get the listing forms and a sign to place in their yard.

It happened that this new agent kept blank forms with him all the time. He was ready for business, and the other agent was not. That is why the other agent lost a listing and eventually a sale. He learned a valuable and costly lesson that day. I bet he will never make the same mistake again.

This brings up a very important point. What should your relationship be with competitor sales agents? I always had ambivalent feelings toward them, because they are competitors. You may hate it when they get a listing you were working on or sell a house to one of your potential buyers.

On the plus side, there will be times they will produce a buyer for your listing. It may be the very listing that was going to expire in a few days, and you would have gotten nothing.

It is pretty nice to come home from vacation to find one of your listings sold, and you made a couple of thousand dollars while vacationing. That is nice even if it was sold by a competitor agent. That has happened to me more than once.

It is much better to have other agents showing and selling your listings, rather than avoiding them, because they do not like to deal with you. Sometimes a buyer is trying to decide between two houses. You do not want the agent to persuade the buyer to buy the other house because he would rather not sell one of your listings.

If you have a run-in with a competitor sales agent, no matter how right you are, don't be too anxious to tell him off. To do so may make you feel good for the moment. However, think of how he will feel. He probably will justify in his own mind why it happened and never accept the fact that it was his fault.

You may make him an adversary for life who will bad-mouth you all over town for the rest of your selling career.

Make friends with competitor agents. It should be easy to do, because you have something in common. Always be fair and friendly, it is the right thing to do. There are other compelling reasons as well. If you are selling real estate, hopefully it will be a life long career.

You may one day own a real estate company and want those fellow competitors to join your team and work for you. Therefore, never burn your bridges with anyone just because they are your competitor. Make friends with them; they are your competitor, not your enemy.

Remember, you are building for the future. Always look ahead in everything you do. In every transaction, sale, listing, etc. Always think about how it can and will impact your future sales.

### Wisdom Nugget 31: Choosing an Attorney

I am going to make a couple of profound statements. Here they are: Most buyers buy, because they want to buy, and most sellers sell, because they want to sell! Is that not profound? That being the case, 90% of the time there is no need for paperwork.

However, there is always that 10%. That is why we have contracts. If a problem or disagreement arises we refer back to the paperwork or contract. Make sure your contracts are clear and not lacking in specificity. That means the contract should be exact and clearly state the terms of the sale or listing.

As a real estate salesman, you are not allowed to practice law. That means you cannot write a contract. For the most part you will use "fill in the blank" contracts and listing forms that were written by attorneys. If you are a REALTOR®, these forms are usually furnished by your state association.

At times you may have to use special stipulations. In many cases, before the contract is signed, you should have these stipulations reviewed by the closing attorney. That brings into play, choosing and dealing with attorneys.

You will have considerable influence over which attorney your customer will use. Choose one that will be helpful to you. Attorneys are trained to be cautious. That is fine as long as they are not overly cautious. Trust me when I say an overly cautious or arrogant attorney can kill your deal.

That is why you need to choose an attorney that is knowledgeable, friendly, and optimistic. You want one that will help you make your creative deals work, not one to tell you all the reasons they will not. You should choose one that specializes in real estate closings.

Avoid attorneys that are arrogant and overly impressed with themselves. It really bothers some of them when you have a closing and walk out the door with several thousand dollars when they only received $600. They are not aware of all the trouble, expense, effort, and time it took you to get to the closing table.

When you interview your attorney, let him know you are in a position to refer many clients to him. Tell him what you expect. Let him know there may be times a big deal is on the line, and you may need legal advice. Tell him it could happen after hours or on a weekend. Let him know it will seldom happen, and you will not bother him unnecessarily.

Tell him if a problem arises at closing, he should help to solve the problem without blaming whoever caused it. I once had an attorney whose ego was so big he could not accept the fact that he had made a mistake so he blamed someone else. I said "goodbye" to that attorney.

Obviously you do not want that kind of attorney. If the attorney you interview is not in agreement with your requirements, choose a different one. You may have to find a young attorney just starting his career. Some of the more established ones may want to dictate the terms of your relationship.

### Wisdom Nugget 32: Be Likable

Much of selling and buying is emotional. People

mostly buy because of emotion rather than necessity. Even when they are buying out of necessity, it helps if the buyer likes you. That is why it is important to make a friend of the buyer.

Never argue even if you are right, and they are wrong. You may win the argument but lose the sale.

### Wisdom Nugget 33: The Depressed Market

The market is cyclical. That means sometimes the market will shrink, and there are fewer sales to be made. Other salesmen around you will be discouraged. However, this is not a time for discouragement. You are needed more than ever.

This is when you have to think and become creative. Look for alternate ways to finance, such as Farmer's Home Loans, Second Mortgages, Wrap Mortgages, Land Sale Contracts, Bartering, etc. This can be a time for you to have your best year ever. Since the pie is smaller, you will have to get a larger slice.

### Wisdom Nugget 34: Agree With Your Customer

If your position is opposite that of your customer, sympathize with them before trying to sell them on a different opinion. This is one of those replies you could work on until it becomes instinctive. Learn to say: "I know how you feel. I felt that way too until I found out..." After you say that, you can go into your selling mode.

### Wisdom Nugget 35: Face Your fears

We all have irrational fears and phobias. Facing and overcoming these fears are important in selling as well as life in general. Usually the biggest fear a salesman has is closing. That's because that's when he gets rejection.

Another fear may be making a speech or speaking in a

crowd. There are many other fears, a fear of the dark, a fear of dying, a fear of ill health, etc. There are grown intelligent adults who will not see a doctor for fear of what the doctor may say.

The first step in overcoming your fears is to recognize and face them. The next step is to learn all you can about the fear. For instance, if it is a fear of closings, learn to overcome objections

Do this by anticipating as many objections as you can think of, then practice by role playing with another sales agent, a friend, or your spouse. Know what you are going to say and do until you become comfortable in closing the sale.

If you fear making a speech, learn the subject matter so thoroughly you will not even need notes. Also, practice in front of a mirror until it becomes natural. Record your practice sessions on video or audio, and critique it. This will give you confidence. I know this works, because I once had both those fears.

Charlie Cullens was a believer of facing and conquering your fears. He tells a story of how he conquered one of his.

When he was a senior in high school, he was captain of the football team. He said he developed a strong attraction for girls, and there were few of them out in the country where he lived. Therefore, he would hang around town after school and fraternize.

When it was time to go home, he had to hitchhike a ride about four miles down the highway to a dirt road which led to his house. He had to walk another mile down that dirt road. Over the years the trees had grown over it making a canopy causing it to be pitch black at night. He always made sure to leave in plenty of time to get home before dark.

Charlie had a couple of problems. First, he was afraid of the dark. The bigger problem was if his teammates found out, he would be the laughing stock, because he was the big football star. Therefore, he decided to conquer that fear.

One day, he purposely waited until dark before hitching a ride. He did it so he would have to walk down that pitch black road. He said after a while he could walk down it whistling. He conquered that fear.

Years later every time he was visiting home, he always made an excuse to walk down that road after dark, knowing he had conquered that fear years ago.

You too can face and conquer your fears. It will make your life richer, more exciting, and a lot less stressful.

### *Wisdom Nugget 36: Open House*

It is a common practice to hold an open house in properties listed to sell. It is important, and I have sold many houses as a result. In almost all cases, the buyer bought a different house from the one they came to see. In a period of over 35 years, only twice did a buyer come to my open house and buy that house.

Many sellers will want you to have an open house on their property as soon as you list it. As a Super Salesman you will have a very large inventory of properties to sell, and it may not be practical to have open house on all of them. Therefore, you must educate the seller as to the purpose of an open house.

Tell the seller the purpose is to attract buyers, the more the better. The house you select to hold open should be based on the features you believe will attract the largest number of potential buyers. Let the seller know you may have a better chance of attracting a buyer for their house by holding an open house someplace else.

I have come to the conclusion that the main purpose

of holding an open house is not to sell the house being held open but to attract as many buyers as possible. Of course, you would like to sell it to someone who attends your open house if you can, but only if it appeals to the buyer and meets his requirements. Every market is different, therefore I cannot say that's true everywhere.

### Wisdom Nugget 37: Facts, Features & Benefits

When telling your customer about a fact or a feature of a property, you should sell the benefit. For example, you say a house has extra insulation. That is a fact. The benefit is it will keep your house warmer in the winter, cooler in the summer, and your power bill will be lower.

Elmer Wheeler, who has been called the greatest salesman in the world, wrote a book titled: *Tested Sentences That Sell.* In it he tells not what the product is but what the product will do. One sentence was, "Sell the sizzle, not the steak." I believe you should sell both "sizzle" and "steak."

Here are some facts and features with their benefits. Fact: The property is near the hospital. Benefit: In case there is an emergency you could get there quickly.

Feature: The house has an underground lawn sprinkler system. Benefit: Have a beautiful lawn without a lot of work and expense. Feature: The property has a well and pump. Benefit: Have all the water you need without a lot of expense.

Feature: The property has a pool. Benefit: Cool off on a hot summer day, also a great place for the kids or grandchildren to play. Or, you can invite your friends for a cool pool party, etc. Feature: The house has a fireplace. Benefit: It would be warm, snug, cozy, and romantic on a cold winter night, plus it can save money on your heating bill.

You can build a repertoire of benefits. Every time you show a house or property and point out a feature, think of what the benefit would be of having that feature. Write it down, and in a short period of time you will have a long list of benefits to fit the feature of almost any house you show.

### Wisdom Nugget 38: Looks Can Be Deceiving

Never make the mistake of judging someone by how they look or dress. When I started to write this little wisdom nugget, immediately several stories jumped into my head. I will share two of them. I bet you have a few of your own.

The first is about a young airman I worked with when I was in the Air Force. He was only a one striper, which is next to the lowest enlisted pay grade. He was married and had several small children. He was older with a college degree, even though he looked to be no more than 16. Another thing about him, he had inherited a ton of money from his grandparents.

One day during his lunch break, while in uniform, he decided to go by the local Buick dealership to look at their large new station wagons. He needed the large car because of the size of his family.

Believe it or not, no one would wait on him. Each time he approached a salesman the salesman would turn and go the other way. Finally, when he ran one down, the salesman asked in a very sarcastic manner, "How are you going to pay for it?" He answered, "When I first got here I was planning to pay cash, now I'm not sure I am going to buy at all, at least not here."

I know how he felt. One Saturday I was working around the house in jeans and a T shirt. I needed a bolt so I jumped into my car and headed down to the local hardware store. Along the way listening to my car radio, I passed a Cadillac dealership having a big sale.

My car radio was on and advertising the new Seville Cadillac. I was thinking of buying a Cadillac so I turned into the dealership. The same thing happened to me. No one would wait on me. As I would approach a salesman, he would turn away. I got irritated and left.

When I got home I told my wife about it. She told me to go back another day wearing a suit and tie and see what happens. Later that week I was dressed up for another occasion and decided to go by the dealership while wearing a suit and tie. Sure enough, I had to fight off the salesmen.

Interestingly, a few years earlier I actually bought a new car on a Saturday under almost the exact same circumstances. I had gone to the store for one thing, heard the radio advertising new cars, and it diverted me into their showroom, where I bought a new car.

It works both ways, just because a person dresses nicely and drives a new fancy car doesn't mean he can buy anything. It could mean he is up to his eyeballs in debt. So remember, how people look is only one of many clues about them.

### Wisdom Nugget 39: First Impressions

The old saying is true. "You only get one chance to make a first impression." Evaluate yourself. The first thing the customer sees is "you." So, how do you look?

That doesn't mean you have to wear a suit and tie. It does mean you must be neat, clean, and well groomed. Don't forget your shoes; they should not look like you just shined them with a brick.

You should be friendly but not overly friendly. Do you show knowledge, confidence, and professionalism? Don't become too familiar in the beginning; it may make the customer feel uncomfortable.

Don't assume a person whose name is Lawrence wants to be called "Larry" or James wants to be called "Jim." Everyone named Robert doesn't want to be called "Bob." It can and does offend some people.

### Wisdom Nugget 40: Prioritize Your Day

Someone once said, "If you don't know where you are going, how will you know when you get there?" In order to know where you are going, each day write down the goals you have for the day.

The story was told that in 1890 at a cocktail party, Andrew Carnegie met Frederick Taylor. Taylor was a young man gaining a reputation for helping to organize the workforce. Carnegie told him if he would give him one good idea he could use, he would pay him $10,000.

Taylor told him to make a list each day of the most important things to do that day. He said to prioritize it so the most important item was on the top of the list and least important item at the bottom.

He said, "Even if you don't finish everything on the list for that day, you will have done the most important things." The remaining items can be reshuffled into the list and prioritized for the next day.

Carnegie sent Taylor the $10,000 check. It would be more than $263,000 in today's dollars. Do you realize you just read a quarter of a million dollar idea, and it only cost you the price of this book? A lesson that valuable is certainly worth using today. Use it every day, and it will almost guarantee your success.

Earlier I suggested that you concentrate on one wisdom nugget each week. For this one I make an exception, move it to the top of your list. You should concentrate on it every day from your first day as a salesman. Do it until it becomes a part of your routine every day. This you must do to become a Super Salesman.

## Wisdom Nugget 41: Specificity & Estoppel

Every profession has developed special words that are specific to their profession. If your doctor says your problem is idiopathic, what he is really saying is he doesn't have the foggiest notion what is wrong with you. If he tells his nurse you had a myocardial infarction, you are in trouble. That means you had a heart attack.

Never use the jargon of your profession. In selling you should always be clear and concise using simple words. In real estate, we say estoppel, lien, RESPA, default, discount points, escrow, counteroffer, listing, FSBO, equity, HUD 1, and a whole host of other words. Do not use these words with your customers.

All the words of our profession say a lot. For instance, the words "specificity," "estoppel," and "amortization" says a lot but only if the person you are talking to knows what they mean.

## Wisdom Nugget 42: Who Makes the Decision

If your customer is a couple, usually one of them will make the decision and have the final say. It is not always the one with the dominant personality. You need to find out who it is, because that is the one who has to be sold.

If you ask who it is, chances are you may get an incorrect answer. Oft times one may think they make the decision when in fact it is the other. To find out, listen and think. It will soon become clear.

## Wisdom Nugget 43: Less Is More

There has been considerable research done on decision making. It was discovered when a person had too many choices, it became more difficult for them to make a decision.

That is good news for real estate salesmen or any salesman. I have said before, your time is important and gas is expensive. Therefore, do not think you have to show your customer every available house on your list.

Once I got an offer on one of my listings through another sales agent. The agent told me the customer really liked the house when she first saw it. She said she was sure her customer would make an offer, but she had two more houses on her list to show.

Sure enough when they finished looking at the other two houses, the offer was made on the house I had listed. Can you believe the agent continued to show the other two houses? Once a customer indicates they like a property stop showing and start selling and closing the sale.

### Wisdom Nugget 44: Be Courteous

Often it will be necessary to call your customer. When you do, remember you are interrupting them. Ask for their permission to continue. Ask if they are busy. If they hesitate, assume they are and ask if it would be better if you called back at a later time.

Have you ever been waiting in line and finally it's your turn? You start talking to the person who is helping you and their phone rings? They answer and start talking. Sure you have. Isn't that annoying? It is also rude.

When you are talking to someone face to face, they are ahead of everyone else. No one and no phone call should ever take precedence over them, except real emergencies. If your phone rings, you could push it to voice mail, or tell the person on the phone you are busy, and they can hold on, or you will call them back.

If they choose to hold on, lay the phone down, and

don't worry about that call until you finish with your customer. If they hang up, it's not the end of the world. They can call back, or you can call them.

Do the same if you are interrupted by someone in the office. That is unless you can give a quick short answer such as "Yes," "No," "Maybe," or "I don't know." Tell them you will talk to them as soon as you finish with your customer.

### Wisdom Nugget 45: They Are Not Bird Dogs

A Center of Influence is that rare person that will help you succeed. It is someone who has lots of time on their hands and likes to know everything going on in their neighborhood.

Some "Centers of Influence," but not all, have been called "nosy neighbors." When you come across such a person, you could tell them to keep their ears and eyes open, and let you know what is going on with their circle of friends.

Periodically call, and ask if they know anyone who is going to sell or buy. They need their ego stroked. So stroke it, and they will be invaluable to you in giving you referrals. Tell them how much you appreciate them. Occasionally take them to lunch, buy them a Christmas present, or give them a gift on their birthday. It will be about the best promotion you could ever do.

Several times in this book I have mentioned "Centers of Influence." It is common in the selling industry to call them "bird dogs." I believe that's because they help sniff out new customers. I never liked calling them bird dogs. I like to call them "Centers of Influence."

### Wisdom Nugget 46: Time

Never say you don't have enough time to do

something. When you say you didn't have time to go to the gym, to eat lunch, or anything else, what you mean is it is not a very high priority. If you find yourself using that excuse, maybe you should seriously look at your priorities.

People do what they want to do. Everyone has the same amount of time, 24 hours every day. How you use that time is a different story. I touched on this in an earlier chapter. I am adding it as a nugget, because it is important to remember.

### Wisdom Nugget 47: Character

You can and should develop your character. Years ago, a friend told me that character is being able to follow through after the emotion subsides. It is not uncommon to be in a small group of your friends, and someone says, "Let's go fishing, golfing, shopping out of town, or whatever."

It is easy to get excited and say "Great, let's do it." Perhaps you did not take into consideration that this commitment may require you to get up at five a.m., instead of when you usually get up at eight.

The next morning when it comes time to roll out of bed, it may not seem like it was such a great idea. How many times have you had plans fall apart, because someone changed their mind? A person of character always does what he says he will do! Your customers expect it and will appreciate you for it.

### Wisdom Nugget 48:  You Earned It, So Keep It

Never be overly fearful of losing a sale. Often in selling real estate, a buyer and seller reach a point where they are only a few hundred dollars apart in making the sale. I have heard salesmen say, "I will just reduce the commission by that amount."

That is something you should never do. If you do, you essentially are saying you are unimportant, and the part you play in making the sale is not important.

Remember, you are the salesman! You are the catalyst! It was you who put the deal together. You are the one who made it happen. You are the important one. You should not become a part of the transaction. If you give up part of your commission, don't be surprised when others find out and expect you to do the same for them.

Once I had a buyer who placed an offer on a house listed with another sales agent. The other agent went with me to present the offer. He was sitting at the table beside me as I presented the offer.

After some negotiating, the buyer and seller were within $100 of making the sale. Suddenly the other agent blurted out, "We will take it off the commission." I gently nudged him with a kick under the table. He immediately said he would take it off his side of the commission.

### Wisdom Nugget 49: Three Nuggets In One

**First Nugget:** When I was about to make an important point I would lightly **touch** my customer's hand or arm to get their attention. Then I would talk **slowly** and **softly**. That was very effective. Often they would lean forward to listen. The touch seemed to make it more personal, and it always had more impact on what I was saying.

**Second Nugget:** One of the sweetest sounds a person hears is the sound of their name. When I first meet someone, if in our conversation they often call my name, it impresses me. If you will think about it, I would bet you have felt the same way when a person often used your name.

It is good advice to use a person's name in all

situations, not just selling. **Especially,** use their name when you say good-bye. People will love you for doing it. That is why it is a good idea to remember your customer's name, and use it in conversation with them. It makes the sale more personal. Remember it is always easier to sell a buyer if they really like you.

**Third Nugget:** Success often comes to those who never give up. Someone once said, "You just can't beat someone who never gives up."

Designations are important to real estate agents; it shows additional training and professionalism.

One designation is Graduate REALTOR® Institute (GRI). In Georgia, it requires a three week course given at Calloway Gardens, held one week each year. It starts with an orientation on Sunday night for approximately 250 students, then classes all week, ending at noon on Saturday.

The third year when I called to sign up, I was told the course was already full, but they would place me on a waiting list. I was number 11 on the list.

When it came time to go, I still didn't have a reservation. Even though it was 200 miles away, I thought someone may drop out, and or some of the alternates may not show up. One of my fellow real estate agents was very loud and vocal as she announced to everyone how stupid it was for me to go.

At the orientation, only one person did not show up and there was an alternate to take his place. So, I decided to stay overnight and show up at the registration the next morning. The agent who announced I was stupid to come, laughed, and reminded me she had told me it was stupid to come without a reservation.

The next morning, everyone showed up, so the agent really got a good laugh, reminding me again how stupid I was as she said, "I'll see you back in Valdosta."

I don't know why, maybe I had a premonition or maybe I just hate to give up, but I felt like something could still happen. Therefore, I hung around for the first class and sat outside the door with it partially open so I could hear the instructor. Some of the officials would walk by and laugh at me. I could see and hear them snickering.

You won't believe what happened next. As the first session ended, one of the students, a diabetic, passed out and fell into the aisle. He partied and drank too much the night before and his sugar got all out of whack. Unfortunately for him, but fortunately for me, he could not continue.

At first they said I could not take his place because I had missed the first class. I reminded them that I sat outside the door with it partially open and had missed nothing. I knew they knew, because they were the ones who snickered at me.

They agreed because they had seen me and couldn't figure out why I was still hanging around. So they allowed me to take the place of the person who had to drop out.

For the rest of the week, the real estate agent who made such a big deal by announcing to everyone and laughing, calling me stupid, was kidded and harassed unmercifully. Almost everyone at the school found out and joined in the kidding.

Making that trip may have been gutsy and not a smart thing to do; but it shows how good fortune comes to those who don't give up and are at the right place at the right time.

### *Wisdom Nugget 50: Never Fear Losing a Sale*

It is interesting how I learned not to fear losing a sale. This is not something you should do. I am just telling you one of my learning experiences. When I was an Air Force recruiter, I worked in a two-man office. I was dealing with mostly young men between 17 and 18 years of age.

Sometimes they would horse around and be rowdy. Other times they would not listen and get up out of their chair and walk around asking question after question that had just been answered. I would very patiently answer their questions over and over, because I was fearful that my prospect might not enlist.

At the height of the Vietnam War, we had just changed from the draft to the all-volunteer force. It was the recruiter's job to make it work. We called it recruiting, but it was really selling.

Being a recruiter was not an easy job at that time, and every recruit was important. It was one of the few jobs in the Air Force where you could be fired if you did not meet your quota. Not meeting quota could cause severe consequences and be detrimental to your career. Because of that, our applicants may have gotten the impression that we were desperate, and we were.

One day my recruiting partner was working with a recruit that was unusually hyper. He ran out of patience, and suddenly with a few expletives thrown in, said to the recruit in an extremely loud and stern voice, "Shut up, and sit down! If you want to go into the Air Force, this is the only way you are going to do it so quit asking questions, and sign here!"

Everyone in the office stopped talking, and it became so quiet you could have heard a feather drop. I thought the young man would either walk or run out the door, but he did neither, instead, he sat down, took the pen and signed. After that, I realized that I did not have to run scared and never again feared losing a sale.

You should never be loud or that harsh with your

customers, even if they are rude and obnoxious. I have seen customers that were very difficult. However, by being very patient and considerate of their feelings, in most cases, even they can be sold.

To me it was always a challenge to try and learn how to work and persuade someone like that to buy or sell. However, if for some reason you can't make the sale, it's not the end of the world. Refer them to another salesman, and perhaps you can get a referral fee.

### Wisdom Nugget 51: What Motivates a Buyer?

What motivates a buyer to buy is a difficult question to answer. Even so, it is something you should think about with every customer. Listen and think! You may be able to answer that question with some of your customers. If you do, it will make the sale much easier.

Once I had a Lieutenant Colonel as a customer; he was transferring to our local Air Force base. He was looking to buy a house without his wife being present. She must have told him not to buy a house unless it had a washer and dryer.

Every house I showed him, he would ask; "Will the washer and dryer stay with this house?" It was early in my selling career. Had I been more experienced, I would have shown him mostly houses where the washer and dryer were part of the sale.

Finally I showed him a small house I thought was below the dignity of a soon to be Commander of an Air Force squadron. Sure enough, like all the other houses, he showed little interest in it. As we started to leave, the owner came home.

He was a First Lieutenant from the local Air Force base. They had something in common and started talking about flying. As they were talking, my customer asked; "If

I buy your house, will you leave the washer and dryer."
The Lieutenant said, "Yes."

I could not believe it; he bought that house. I went home and told my wife he paid $70,000 for a washer and dryer. The house was just thrown in as a bonus.

### *Wisdom Nugget 52: A Short Lesson On Money*

As a Super Salesman you will be investing as well as working with investors. Therefore, it is important to understand the concept of money.

It is a medium of exchange and has a time value. Money itself has very little intrinsic value. Intrinsically, its highest and best use would probably be as kindling to start a fire. However, its true value at any certain time is based on what you can exchange it for at that time.

In 1958 with a stack of twenty $100 bills you could exchange it for a new, black, 58 Ford sedan. I know; I bought one. Or, you could have decided to save the $2,000 for a rainy day. Well, here it is almost 60 years later; you wake up, look out, and see it's raining. Therefore, you decide to spend your $2,000.

You take your stack of twenty $100 dollar bills and head down to the Ford dealership. When you get there you will find you can't exchange it for a new automobile as I did in 1958.

However, if they happen to sell motor scooters and mopeds, you can make an exchange, and at least you won't have to walk home. If you hang onto it for even longer, you may be lucky to exchange it for a bicycle.

It is important to remember this when you make out your will. If you bequest a certain dollar amount, it may be enough to buy an automobile at the time you draw up the will. However, at the time of your death it may only buy a motor scooter or a bicycle.

That is why you may want to consider using percentages based on the income or value of your estate rather than a set dollar amount.

### A Word Of Advice:

The purpose of this book is to teach you the how to of selling. Because I may have had a small influence on your success I feel compelled to give a short word of advice.

When you become a Super Salesman, you will obtain untold riches. If you do it right, a part of your wealth will include the friends and acquaintances you make.

Never think, because you have more money than those around you, you are better than they. You are not! You may be better educated, better at selling, have a more expensive home or car, and all the things that money can buy. Still that does not make you better than anyone else! What good are all those things if no one can stand to be around you?

**Important lessons in this chapter!** Actually, there are 52 of them. Each year get a calendar, and place the numbers one through 52 consecutively on it, a different number for each week.

The first of each week, check to see what number is on the calendar. That is the Nugget you should concentrate on for that week. Continue to do this for the rest of your selling career. As a result, imagine how knowledgeable you will be at the end of your first year of selling and all the years thereafter.

Another thing you could do is to re-read this book every year, not just the 52 Wisdom Nuggets. You can't possibly absorb everything in one reading. Every time you read it, you will probably be surprised at the ideas you missed from the prior reading. It will be like getting more and more new ideas each time you read it.

# CHAPTER TWENTY

## How To Become a Super Salesman

I hope this is the chapter you have been waiting to read. In it will be some more ideas as well as how to apply the ideas you read about earlier in this book.

I will begin by telling you of two regrets I have in my life. I do not dwell on them, but I do think of them from time to time. Neither is important.

The first regret is very insignificant and you may even think it silly. It involved the last play of the last football game during my senior year of high school.

The coach sent me into the game, and told me to tell the quarterback to call a "61." It was a dumb play to call. We had used it all night and never made any yardage. However, there was a variation of it called a "61 reverse."

It was a trick play. It was the same play except a reverse was added. As in the "61," the ball was snapped to me instead of the quarterback. However, instead of handing it off, I would fake the handoff, keep the ball and run in the opposite direction. It had not been used in that game, so the other team wouldn't have anticipated it.

We were losing about 20 to nothing, and it was the last play of the game. We could not have won no matter what play was called. Therefore, it didn't really matter. Even though the coach said to call the "61", I almost told the quarterback to call a "61 reverse." I didn't change the play, and sure enough the runner was tackled behind the line of scrimmage for a loss, and the game was over.

I often wonder what would have happened had I told the quarterback to call a "61 reverse." In my mind I see myself, as my team's hero, streaking down the sidelines for our only touchdown of the game. Oh well! In a moment

I will tell why I told that story.

Now back to business. My success as a salesman was well above average. I far exceeded the financial goals I had set out to obtain. I suppose I could be called a "minor" Super Salesman. Looking back I now realize that, **with no more effort**, I could have been a real Super Salesman. Chances are, so can you!

I was successful from the very beginning. My first month I sold five houses, and my success continued on from there. Even so, upon reflection, I realize I didn't reach my full potential of becoming a Super Salesman.

It wasn't that I would have had to work harder. It was partly because without realizing it, I had conditioned myself to not go beyond the goal I had set. After I reached my goal each year, I worked the same amount of time but didn't seem to accomplish very much.

I suppose I was satisfied. This prevented me from becoming a salesman to the maximum of my capability. That is my second regret. As a part of that regret, I wish I would have met Stanley Mills earlier in my career. He was a Super Salesman who I will discuss later in this chapter.

In some ways, it is unfortunate that when I met him I was an Owner/Broker. I still did some selling and used some of the ideas I learned from him. But by this time, much of what I did was working with and training my sales agents.

I mention these two regrets to say you do not get a "do-over." There are no "mulligans" in life. We all have to live like we are playing a professional game: by the rules.

If we do not play by the rules of life, we will be penalized, sometimes severely. For instance, there is a rule about gravity; it is called the "law of gravity." If you violate it by jumping off a tall building or even if someone pushes you and it is not your fault, the rule still applies. "Splat!"

Try stopping a speeding car or a bullet with your body. You will not like the outcome. Fall off a boat in the middle of the ocean without a life jacket and you will drown. That is, unless a shark eats you first.

These are the rules of life. You have no option; you must abide by them. There is no "do over," therefore, it is imperative that you get it right the first time.

I know by sharing my 40 plus years of selling experience with you, it will help you to reach your goal of becoming a Super Salesman. I hope this book will help you to do it right the first time. That is because when you retire you can't go back and get a "do over." If you do it right, you will have no regrets.

Before we get into the meat of this chapter, let's talk about the obstacles that could keep you from reaching your goal of becoming a Super Salesman. More importantly you need to learn how to overcome those obstacles.

One of the biggest impediments I see is that you may have conditioned yourself for failure in certain areas without being aware of it! Even though I saw it in others, I was unaware that I had also conditioned myself in a few negative ways.

For example, when I reached a certain level of income each year, even if it was in September, I would slow down for the rest of the year. I had reached my goal. Therefore it was time to play. Maybe it was golfing, fishing, hunting, or going on vacations.

Once, I talked my wife into helping me do a lot of my paperwork and take phone calls so I would have more time to sell. It turned out I didn't sell more. I just played more, so she said, "You're on your own; I'm out of here."

I was unaware I had conditioned myself to be comfortable after I had reached a certain level of income.

It was only after I retired and analyzed my selling career, did I realize I had developed this negative conditioning.

There are many scientific experiments that demonstrate the phenomenon of conditioning. One is called The Pike Syndrome experiment. Another involves fleas.

Recently I wrote an article and it was published in the local newspaper. In it, I mentioned those two experiments to make my point clear. I asked the readers to go onto the INTERNET, and watch the videos of the experiments.

As people would speak to me about the article, I would ask them if they watched the videos of the experiments. Not one person had watched them. That was too bad, because they missed much of the point I was trying to make.

This next lesson I will discuss is extremely important. Therefore, don't be like those people. Stop reading right now and look both these videos up on the INTERNET. Watch "The Pike Syndrome" and "Fleas in a Jar."

Pay close attention to them. The videos have extremely important **life changing** lessons to be learned. That is why you need to stop reading and watch them. The messages in them can make the difference of whether you will become a Super Salesman or just a mediocre or average salesman.

I am going to explain those experiments in the event for some reason you cannot view them because your computer is broken or something else. As you will see in the first experiment, a great northern pike is placed into a large fish tank filled with water. A large clear glass jug with the bottom cut off is inserted straight down into the water.

The top of the jug was off when it was inserted into the tank so it would fill with water. About a dozen minnows are inserted through the opening in the top of the jug. They could swim around but were confined inside the jug. The Pike could see them while swimming around them in the tank outside the jug.

Minnows are a favorite food of the Pike. Therefore, when one of the minnows got close to the edge of the glass jug, the pike not knowing there was a clear glass barrier between them made a mad dash to get it. Of course, the Pike would bust his mouth and bounce off the glass jug.

Time after time the Pike would attempt to get a minnow, only to bust his mouth every time. Finally, he gave up and swam around the jug totally ignoring the minnows. He never made another attempt to get one.

The next step in the experiment was to lift the glass jug out of the tank. This allowed the minnows out into the tank, and they swam freely around the Pike. However, the Pike ignored them. Day after day the Pike ignored the minnows until he died of starvation. We humans are very much like that Pike.

I am going to say that again. "We humans are very much like that Pike!" For whatever reason, many times we condition ourselves to act in ways that may be detrimental to us in obtaining our goals. We continue to miss opportunities, because we have developed self-imposed barriers.

The other experiment involved fleas. When fleas were inserted into a jar they would jump out through the top. Therefore, the next time the fleas were placed into the jar, a lid was placed on it. As fleas normally do, they jump. When they jumped, they hit themselves on the lid covering the jar and fell back. After a time, they continued to jump but not high enough to hit the lid.

Three days later the lid was removed. After that, the fleas continued to jump; however, for the rest of their lives, they never jumped high enough to jump out of the jar. Interestingly, their offspring wouldn't jump out of the jar either.

They were capable of jumping high enough, but they never did. There are many other conditioning experiments which involve an elephant, a monkey, and other animals. There have been conditioning experiments with humans as well.

It is true; we humans do the same thing. It is called conditioning. Let me explain more about how people condition themselves. Once I recruited a sales agent from another company. Because she was going to have to give up all her listings, I agreed to pay her a commission of 90% for one year to compensate for that loss.

That gave her an opportunity to considerably increase her income from the prior year. However, I noticed when she had obtained the approximate income of the prior year, she became a "not worker." She would roam the halls looking for someone to carry on a conversation. I found that interesting, not realizing I had developed a similar problem.

Once I read about a professional golfer who had an outstanding start in a golf tournament. After three days, he was ahead by four strokes. Before going into his last day of the tournament he was interviewed on TV. At the interview he said, "I may not win tomorrow, but I have given the big boys a scare."

Talk about being conditioned for failure and lack of confidence! It sounded like he was already rehearsing his speech for when he loses the next day. Sure enough, the next day he had a bad start and lost the tournament by several strokes. The author of the book said, "Now he's happy, he is back in the pack."

Here is another example of how conditioning can

affect a person. Jean van de Verlde, a Frenchman and professional golfer had a five-shot lead at the start on the final day at the 1999 British Open at Carnoustie. He had an opportunity to become the first Frenchman to ever win a British Open or any other Open. It would have been history in the making.

Before he started the last day, he told the press he was surprised to be ahead by five-strokes. What he was really saying is he didn't feel comfortable being in that lofty position. By the time he got to the last hole, he was down to a three shot lead. Imagine that, only one hole to go and a three shot lead.

With a three shot lead at the last hole, even I could have played that hole and won the tournament for him. He had really conditioned himself for failure. As a result, he figured out a way to lose the tournament.

The lesson here is to never ever set a limit on what you can achieve. If you approach your goal, increase it each time you approach it. The sky is the limit. Now for a note of caution, be wary when you show or tell your goals. Many of your friends or relatives may try to discourage you.

To change and avoid conditioning yourself for failure, you must recognize areas where you are weak. Think about it. You are intelligent, so periodically analyze yourself.

If you are not obtaining or exceeding more than others around you, ask yourself why? You are not looking for excuses. You are looking for reasons. If you know the reason, it will not take long to recognize the areas that you need to strengthen.

If you are already conditioned in a negative way, the way to change yourself is to first recognize your weaknesses. That is more than half the battle. Then change yourself by setting and achieving realistic goals.

Remember to adjust those goals upwards as you approach them. Do not be afraid to rise to any challenge that presents itself. Work the expensive, as well as the inexpensive properties, the highly educated, as well as the uneducated customers.

Purposely force yourself to step outside your comfort zone. For example, many new sales agents feel more comfortable working less expensive properties.

They may feel that owners or buyers of million dollar properties are more knowledgeable than they. Little do they know those owners may be less knowledgeable about real estate than someone who owns an inexpensive property.

Because these new agents have been selling real estate for a short time, their confidence level may be low. Or, it could be that many of the agents are conditioned on a subconscious level to feel they are only entitled to a certain level of income.

To change, you must step outside the box. Use your intellect to force yourself to do things you feel uncomfortable doing. You will feel more comfortable doing them after your emotional side accepts these changes.

You may be surprised, even shocked to find that many times those expensive properties, you were so worried about, turn out to be easier to list or sell than the inexpensive ones.

To overcome negative conditioning, start out by setting goals. Write down each goal. One could be to make a certain amount of income in a year. Be realistic, set an obtainable goal.

If you have never earned more than $40,000 in a year, do not set a goal of $1,000,000. Once you see you are approaching your goal, increase it. Change your goal in writing. Remember, the sky is the limit, just be realistic.

In order to obtain your income goal, you should determine how many listings or sales you will need in order to reach that goal. You can further break it down into how many listings per week. Make that one of your goals. Always write down your goals, and review them to see if you are on track or if they need to be increased.

Once you set a goal, never give up on it. Strive hard to achieve it! Once I called a young man I knew at 11 p.m. on a Saturday night, because I was one short of my goal of listings for the month. As a result, I reached my goal. That is the kind of tenacity you need.

In a paragraph above, I stated as you are about to reach your goal, increase it. Here is an example of why you should do that. I do not recall his name, but I will tell the story anyway.

Many years ago, a professional football player predicted to the press and anyone else who would listen, that he would catch 100 passes the next year. Although he had never done that before, he believed he could do it and was determined.

He told all the players. He wrote it on a note and stuck it on his locker. He told all his family, neighbors, and friends. He stuck a note on his bathroom mirror and even stuck notes all around in his house.

Sure enough, in the last game of the next season, he caught his 100th pass. They stopped the game and presented him with the football. The game then resumed and he was tossed a short pass right into his hands; he dropped it. He also dropped the next one.

He had reached his goal; therefore, his subconscious told him there was no need to catch another pass. Had he adjusted his goal upward, chances are he would have caught those two passes. Isn't it strange how the mind works?

At this point, you should know many of the elements of becoming a Super Salesman. Let's go over a few of them. Analyze yourself to be sure you have not conditioned yourself for failure in any area.

Make realistic goals, and write down each one. Review and adjust them upward as you approach each goal. Not only write down the goals, even write down the upward adjustments.

Never give up on any one of your goals. Strive to achieve them. Get organized and stay organized! Constantly promote yourself! Hire assistants to do the mundane task, so you can do what is most important; that is being face to face with buyers and sellers. Be a student by always being in a learning mode. Embrace technology, and use it to accomplish your goals.

Now I am going to tell you about Stanley Mills, a real Super Salesman. Before I tell you about him, let me tell you how it came about that we met.

Our youngest daughter, her husband, and our two grandsons were living in the Memphis, Tennessee area. Once or twice a year, my wife and I would go out for a visit. It was a two-day trip each way, so we always planned to visit for about ten days to two weeks.

It was on one of those trips that I noticed many, many Crye-Leike real estate signs the closer we got to Memphis. I assumed they were the largest company in that region. After several days of visiting with everyone, I got restless and decided to go to the home office of Crye-Leike and talk to some of their real estate agents.

Their home office was on the outskirts of Memphis, Tennessee bordering Germantown. When I pulled up to the building I was very impressed. It was five stories tall and had an all glass front and was 100,000 square feet in area. I thought they must be doing something right.

I went into the building and told the receptionist I was a real estate broker from South Georgia and wanted to talk to some of their agents. As a matter of fact, I told her I would like to talk to their top salesman.

She introduced me to Stanley Mills, their number one salesman. He had sold and closed over 19 million dollars in residential sales the year before, earning almost a million dollars in commission income.

I told him I wanted to follow him around for a couple of days and pick his brain. I said I would buy his lunch, and he graciously accepted my offer. For the next two days, I was Stanley's shadow around his office. It is unbelievable how much I learned in those two days

Let me describe Stanley. He was approaching middle age and was a little overweight. Because he was a diabetic, he did not appear to be in the best physical condition. He was a very friendly sort of person. As I got to know and listen to him talking to his customers on the phone, I didn't think his selling skills were any better than mine.

Strangely, he did not seem to work any longer or harder than I did. He wasn't selling million dollar homes; they were only slightly more expensive than the homes I was selling. He was not a tall, dark, and handsome charismatic silver tongue orator.

So, why did he have 19 million dollars in sales the year before, and I only had slightly over a million? That was a mystery, and I had to get to the bottom of it.

One thing I noticed about him. He didn't appear to be greedy. He wasn't driven to get every listing and make every sale possible. As a matter of fact, he would let his customers know if they wanted to buy a house from "Stanley Mills" it wouldn't be on a Saturday morning. That was his morning to play golf.

As I just now gave my assessment and description of Stanley, it wasn't to make any kind of bad reflection on him. It was to let you know he was just an ordinary guy. To me, he is a prime example that you do not have to be extraordinary to be an extraordinary salesman. **You can be just like Stanley!**

Another thing I noticed, he was extremely organized and focused. That may have come about because he had a degree in accounting. I once knew another real estate salesman who had been an accountant. He also was very successful, although not nearly as successful as Stanley.

Computers were not as powerful in the mid-nineties as they are today. However, even then, there were good contact programs available that were designed specifically for real estate. A contact program is an excellent tool for keeping you organized. I am sure today they are even more sophisticated than they were back in the mid-nineties when I met Stanley.

These contact programs are available for real estate as well as many other areas of sales. If you cannot find one that suits you, give a young college kid or geek a few bucks to convert an accounting software program to specifically suit your requirements.

I hope when you read the last two paragraphs you did not skim over them. Of all the good ideas in this book, I believe the contact program is one of, if not the most important tool for a salesman. If you do not get one and learn to use it, you may never reach your full potential as a Super Salesman.

Remember, as a Super Salesman, you will have so many irons in the fire you cannot possibly keep up with everything. You will need help, and the contact program is that help. It will make it all so simple. Therefore, I believe that using a good contact program will have as much or more impact on your success than anything else you will do.

Now back to Stanley. He had a small one-man office. Right next to his office was the office of his secretary. The door was always open between them. There was no need for an intercom. They were in normal talking distance of one another, probably no more than eight feet apart.

When the phone rang the secretary would answer and tell Stanley who was on the phone. Before he would answer, he turned around to his computer. He would pull up the name on his contact list to see if he had previously worked with him. It only took him a moment. After he read his notes he answered the phone.

If Stanley had previously talked to him and he had told Stanley he was going to plant a garden, it would be in his notes. If so, he would say something like: "Hi Jim, are the beans ready to be picked?" Before he hung up, he would ask; "who do you know on your street that's thinking of selling their house?"

Maybe he would say, "How was the vacation in Florida?" Maybe it would be, "How is the grandson?" It was usually about something he had in his notes; then he would ask for business.

After their conversation, he would make new notes on the computer about what they had just discussed. That way, the next time he got a call from Jim or any of his many other customers, he could take up right where he had left off the last time they had talked. His customers must have thought he had a great memory.

It takes extraordinary discipline to always make notes on your computer after every conversation, and that was something he always did.

Stanley had a list of anniversaries, birthdays, other

special situations, occasions, and projects of his customers. His computer had an appointment calendar and every day it would remind him of those birthdays, anniversaries, etc.

He would call each one and say something like, "Hi Jim, tomorrow is your anniversary. Don't forget to get your wife some flowers. If you forget, your wife may have me out there the next day to place your house on the market to sell."

Always, before he hung up, he would ask for business and make notes. I didn't see Stanley do this, but I suspect if he was extremely busy, sick, or on vacation, he would let his secretary or one of his assistants make the call to recognize special occasions of his customers.

We have talked about setting goals and being organized. Now I am going to give you some of the ideas I got from Stanley on how to promote yourself.

He told me one day he was driving down the Interstate and noticed a picture of a Cadillac on a billboard. It happened that he bought a Cadillac from that very dealer almost every year.

When he saw the sign, he turned around and headed to the dealership. He reminded the dealer he bought a Cadillac from him almost every year. He also told him their billboard would have more credibility if a well known satisfied customer was saying to buy a Cadillac from them.

They agreed, and sure enough, when I drove down the Interstate, I saw it. There it was; the billboard had a picture of my Super Salesman leaning against a Cadillac.

The caption under the picture said something like: "STANLEY MILLS OF CRYE-LEIKE REAL ESTATE SAYS, BUY A CADILLAC FROM. . ." That was worth thousands of dollars per month in self-promotion, and it didn't cost him anything. Remember how I have said you need to be constantly thinking? This is a perfect example of what can happen if you will just think.

On a table in his office, I saw a magazine that said "Stanley's Magazine." It had page after page of pictures with descriptions and prices of the houses he had listed for sale. Sometimes a house would sell after the picture was sent to the publishing company. In that case, if it was past the deadline, he would call them, and they would stamp "Sold" across the face of the picture.

The magazine had some light and interesting reading articles, jokes, cartoons, recipes, etc. I do not recall if the picture of the Cadillac billboard was in the magazine, but it could have been. You can design yours, and place into it whatever pictures you want. I asked him about the magazine, and he explained it was all free. That got my attention!

He said, "If you notice, there are ads in the back portion of the magazine." He further stated that he sold many builders' houses. Those builders worked with many subcontractors, such as electricians, plumbers, painters, carpenter framers, and carpet/vinyl contractors.

In addition, he referred a considerable amount of business to banks and attorneys. They are the ones who paid for the magazine by placing their ads in it.

Most of them were glad to do so, because they knew Stanley helped their business by selling the houses. They knew if it helped him, it would help them. As long as he sold houses, the builders would continue to build others. In addition, the subcontractors, bankers, and attorneys knew his magazine would get a wide distribution and help them in their business.

Stanley told me there were companies that publish those magazines. All he had to do was line up the advertisers and send in pictures with descriptions of the houses he wanted inserted into the magazine. They would take care of everything else. Each month he would receive several hundred magazines, free.

He would then have them distributed to the lobbies and waiting rooms of banks, doctors' offices, attorneys' offices, insurance offices, motels, etc. Notice I said he had them distributed to those places.

He didn't have time to do it all by himself. He had his assistant distribute them, as well as do all the leg-work in putting the magazine together. As a matter of fact, I think he had two assistants besides his secretary.

When I got back home, I developed a magazine that I called "Hoot's Magazine." Like Stanley, it didn't cost me anything. So, I know it works.

Something else I learned from Stanley is to always do what is most productive. That is to be face to face with buyers and sellers.

You can hire someone to do those other necessary requirements of selling, whether it is real estate, insurance, or anything else requiring paperwork. For instance after you list a house, pictures must be taken. The house must be measured. A description of the house, such as the number of bedrooms and baths will be needed for the Multi-List system.

There is a considerable amount of information required before the Multi-List system will place it on the market to sell. Also, it should be posted on the INTERNET.

For the houses already sold but not yet closed, someone needs to coordinate and follow-up with the bank, appraiser, and attorney to make sure there is nothing that will delay the closing. That is important work, but Stanley did not need to do it.

As you become more successful, you will need to hire

an assistant to do this time consuming work. You can hire a secretary and/or assistant at minimum wage or slightly higher.

You should work a commission into their pay scale so they will have the incentive to be competent, accurate, and help you to increase your sales. Since you are paying them a commission that means their pay goes up only if your sales increase. The more their pay increases the better.

It will take some of your time, but you absolutely must train your secretary and assistant. They will be your competent right arm. As your business grows, you may need to hire more than one assistant.

At that point, your assistant can train your new employee. As a Super Salesman, your time is extremely valuable. Let your secretary or assistant do those necessary things that must be done after the sale is made.

You can work for a company that requires you to pay a monthly dollar fee to place your license with them. Or, you can own and be a broker of your own company. If that will take too much of your time, you may decide to work for an already established company like Stanley did.

If you do, it should be a company with a sliding commission scale. The scale should go up to 90% or higher. If you have earned your company $50,000 to $70,000 in a year that will be more than most agents will earn them.

That means the commissions you earn above each set point will pay you a higher percentage. That's important because at some point, you will be hiring and paying your own secretary and assistants.

On the other hand, there would be fewer regulations and paperwork for you if your company would agree to pay your secretary and assistants. In which case, of course, your commission percentage will not go as high. One other thing you should consider. Negotiate in advance what will happen to your listings if you ever decide to leave the company.

There you have it. Find your own Super Salesman, and do what I did. Call around to the large companies in or outside of your area, and try to find a salesman that does at least 15 million dollars a year in sales. Hopefully you can find one who will allow you to follow him around for several days.

Make this a top priority. Assure him you will not interfere or get in his way. Let him know you will be as quiet as a church mouse. You could even tell him perhaps one day you will write a book and dedicate one chapter to him as I did about Stanley. (Just joking)

Hopefully one of them will be flattered and allow you to follow them the way Stanley did for me. You could do this every few years. Even a time, as little as two days will do more for your career than you could ever imagine.

I keep saying him, but it could be him, or her. Now for a few last points, it is known that approximately 80% of all sales are made by 20% of the sales force. To be a Super Salesman, you will need to be in the top 20% of that 20% which would place you in the top 4% in the nation.

Ask yourself if you are willing to learn and do what will place you into that top 4%. To become a Super Salesman, you must **really, really WANT** it. It has to be a different kind of **want. It should be a passion that will consume your thinking**.

You must have confidence and faith in yourself. The Bible says "If ye have faith as a grain of mustard seed, ye shall say unto this mountain, Remove hence to yonder place; and it shall remove; and nothing shall be impossible unto you."

In another place it says, "Even so faith, if it hath not

works, is dead..." Therefore, if you have the faith to move a mountain, you had better get on a bulldozer and start pushing. There is a lot of wisdom and good selling philosophy in the Bible.

Almost everyone **wants** to be highly financially successful but without effort. That is why hundreds of millions of dollars are squandered on the lottery every year.

That is not the kind of **want** I am talking about. Everyone wants success. I am talking about a passion, a yearning that cannot be satisfied until you succeed. Fortunately, you cannot fail to succeed if you do what you will have learned in this book.

One last thought. Work hard, study hard, learn, and persevere. Everything you need to know is right here before you. Remember, working hard is not working hard if you enjoy what you are doing. Someone once said if you love your job, you will never work a day in your life.

I hope you are ready to start on this most exciting adventure. Every day will be more fun and exciting than the day before. If you really, really want to be a Super Salesman, it will be easy... and hard! But you can and will love doing it.

Approach it like the beginning of a thousand mile hike; you start by taking one step at a time. You have the resources and guide to begin and you can complete the journey. Just start taking those steps, one at a time. **THE REST IS UP TO YOU!**

It is now time to go back and re-read the last four paragraphs of the Introduction. It is also time for you to start learning by doing. If you will discipline yourself and put into practice what you will have learned in this book, one day you will be one of the top salesmen in America, **A SUPER SALESMAN!**

# EPILOGUE

This is a "how to" book. You should not just read it. You should study and revisit it throughout your selling career. I assure you every time you read it, you will pick up new ideas that you missed or forgot the last time you read it.

Even though I feel this is an excellent guide and tool to assist you in reaching your goal of becoming a Super Salesman, do not forget to take advantage of other resources I have mentioned.

As a reminder, attend seminars, read motivational, and training books. The names of a few are mentioned in this book, but there are many others and you can find them on the INTERNET. Also, brainstorm with other successful salespeople. Listen and watch sales training and motivational tapes and videos.

Over time some of my memories may have faded. Some great ideas surely have been forgotten. That is OK, because you will discover them on your own. I could not possibly write about everything you will need to know and do.

Now you have an excellent tool and guide to help you as you begin this exciting adventure. The concepts and ideas here will help you to succeed beyond your wildest imagination. As time goes by you may be able to add a few chapters of your own.

If you do the things you will have learned in this book, your success will be assured and it will not be nearly as hard as you think! And yet!... It may be harder but lots of fun.

The main thing is to do what you now know to do. Go and do what Napoleon Hill said. **See the People!... See the People!... See the People!...** And when you see them you will know what to say and what to do. So, get started! **YOU CAN DO IT!!!**

# ACKNOWLEDGMENT

I want to thank all the buyers, sellers, and the many sales agents I have worked with over the years. Those people are the real heroes of this book. They are the ones who made the book possible.

Especially, I want to thank Stanley Mills who allowed me to be his shadow and follow him around for two days. What a learning experience that was.

I thank my wife, Sybil, for her many hours of editing. Fortunately, she has a better knowledge of the English language than I. Sometimes the writing of my thoughts didn't flow very smoothly, and she helped to make them flow better. Without her help, the reading of this book would have been much more difficult.

In addition, I want to thank her for allowing me to annoy her when I would ask her opinion about an idea I had. I also thank her for the many times throughout my career she had to adapt to my unorthodox schedule.

Another person I want to thank is Joe V. "Bud" Dasher, Jr., for the many years of our friendship and his encouragement, as well as editing. Even though his name is not mentioned, he was a participant in several of my learning experiences and at least one of the stories in this book. In addition, he contributed the Prologue and an endorsement on the back cover.

**Editing**: I especially thank Connie Noffer, for the many hours of time spent doing an outstanding job of editing; Larry Mercer gave invaluable help as well; Others who helped in editing were; attorney Kari Anne Bowden; Robert Boyce of SmartCarry®, "The invisible holster;" Paul Guilbeau of Diamond Realty; Karen Fant and her husband Cochran.

**Computing:** Thanks Clinton "Clint" T. Wynn for being there to answer my many questions or help to find or change a file on my computer; Also, Kevin Pledger, Music Minister at Village of Faith Baptist Church who introduced me to the website "FIVERR;" Heather Walton along with Paul Guilbeau of Diamond Realty who helped with software problems; Debbi Cook also helped with software issues.

**Book Cover:** A thanks to Efe Okhionkpamwonyi Brian who assisted in designing the cover and drew the illustration of the Super Salesman on the front of the book. He can be reached on the INTERNET at: "fiverr.com/users/brianchesky."

**Formatting:** Thanks to Okoeguale Gabriel Oseyi, he can be reached at: "fiverr.com/ose_solutions."

**In addition**, I want to personally thank all the following people. Each in their own special way helped to make this book possible by their input on editing or suggestions to make the reading flow better: My daughters Mechelle Sullivan and Gogi Hinman; My grandson Caleb Bowden; Brandon Tillman, the young man in the gym mentioned in the beginning of the book; Ron Wallace, Associate Pastor at Village of Faith Baptist Church; Dave Curry, who gave an endorsement on the back cover; Zane Horton, a friend; Jane Keel, a friend; Jack A. Riehle, who wrote the Foreword and assisted with software and computer issues; Eileen Beekman, President of The Maximum Group also gave suggestions and editing assistance.

**I hope you enjoyed reading my book. If you have comments, questions, or wish to purchase additional copies, please contact me at *36hoot@gmail.com* or order from *amazon.com***

Hoot, still has fun riding his electric unicycle at age 81